BEHAVIOR SCIENCE TRANSLATIONS

THE MEWU FANTZU

A TIBETAN TRIBE OF KANSU

Hans Stübel

HRAF PRESS NEW HAVEN 1958

The Translation Series is one of several means by which the Human Relations Area Files seeks to promote and facilitate research and comparative study in the sciences concerned with the behavior of men. Other means include the Survey of World Cultures, series of country surveys, behavior science monographs, bibliographies, outlines, and reprints, as well as the Area Files.

Dr. Stübel's manuscript was translated from the German for the Human Relations Area Files by Frieda Schutze. The English manuscript was edited by Shelton Hicock and Mary Rouse.

TABLE OF CONTENTS

TABLE OF CONTENTS

TABLE OF CONTENTS

INTRODUCTION

The present account is based on notes I took on a journey through Kansu in the summer and fall of 1936. The purpose of my trip was to become better acquainted with a Tibetan nomad tribe. Unfortunately, there arose during the trip difficulties I could not foresee. While I was in the Tibetan grassland, Mao Tse-tung's army invaded southern Kansu on its famous long march to the north,[1] and I was forced to break off my work prematurely since I was in danger of being cut off from Lanchow, the capital of Kansu. This march to the north was one portent of the troubled times which began with the Sino-Japanese War and continued with World War II and the Communist revolution in China. In the tumult of this period, I lost both my ethnological collection and the voluminous photographic material I had accumulated. Thus, an essential part of the work I had planned— the illustrations—is lacking. Furthermore, without the objects I had collected, it was impossible to describe the material culture of the tribe I visited as exactly as I should have liked. I therefore refer the reader primarily to the illustrations and excellent brief descriptions made by W. W. Rockhill of his collection in the United States National Museum in Washington.[2] For illustrations of the landscape the reader is referred to Tafel's book on his Tibetan journey, and for ethnic types and folk costumes to Hermanns' work.[3]

In the meantime, our knowledge of the nomads of northeastern Tibet (or Kansu) has increased tremendously. I refer chiefly to the broad general work of Father Hermanns and to R. B. Ekvall's excellent portrayal

---

1. Through South China from Kiangsi to Yunnan, hence through the western border region of China to Kansu, and finally to Yenan in Shensi.

2. William Woodville Rockhill, Notes on the Ethnology of Tibet (Washington, Government Printing Office, 1895).

3. Albert Tafel, Meine Tibetreise (My Tibetan Trip) (Stuttgart: Union Deutsche Verlagsgesellschaft, 1914); Matthias Hermanns, Die Nomaden von Tibet (The Nomads of Tibet) (Vienna, 1949).

of the sociological and economic conditions of the region I visited.[4]
Hermanns gives a survey of Tibetan nomad culture; Ekvall discusses cultural interaction among the Chinese, Moslems, and Tibetans. The latter
work is rich in factual material and is of great interest to the ethno-
sociologist.

The above-mentioned authors had the advantage of living for many
years among the Tibetans and of speaking their language. I can present
only a modest supplement to their work by setting forth my observations of
a single tent camp. Besides my assistant Mr. Wu Hsin-wei, an experienced
ethnological fieldworker, I was fortunate in having as traveling companions
an excellent interpreter and a reliable Chinese-speaking Tibetan to look
after the horses. My interpreter was a Chinese trader who lived in Heh-tso,
the Chinese-Moslem settlement situated nearest the area I visited. As a
young man he had been forced to flee into the region of the Tibetan nomads
during a Moslem uprising and subsequently had lived and traded among
them for many years. He was particularly friendly with some of the Tibetans in the camp I visited. He was a keen observer and apparently was himself interested in the life of the nomads. He was always willing to answer
my questions as objectively as was possible for a simple trader, to arrange
introductions with Tibetan informants, and to interpret patiently.

Since the landscape and climate of the Tibetan steppes have often
been depicted by more competent persons, further description does not
seem necessary here. The weeks I spent in a small tent adjoining the camp
of the Mewu Fantzu were not only a period of ethnological fieldwork but
also an inspiring aesthetic experience. In the height of summer, the steppe
is a gay carpet of flowers, especially edelweiss, bright-blue gentians, and
red and yellow louseworts. From the heights between the shallow valleys
there are limitless vistas in all directions, interrupted only by steep, light-
colored limestone massifs whose 5,000-meter peaks are often covered with
fresh snow. To the south the horizon is blocked by the mighty Min Shan,
a chain of "Matterhorns" with peaks almost 6,000 meters high, glaciers,
and the imposing notch of the "Stone Gate" (Shih-men) that leads to Szechwan. I have memories of long horseback rides, of meditative walks be-
neath the deep-blue alpine sky; and of dark, storm-driven rain clouds in
the solemn peace of the highlands, the quiet broken only by the song of the
larks, the shrill cry of the falcons, the deep caw of the ravens, and the live-
ly whistle of the marmots. I remember the vast, deserted steppe, animated

---

4. Hermanns, ibid.; Robert B. Ekvall, Cultural Relations on the Kansu-
Tibetan Border (Chicago: The University of Chicago Press, 1939).

now and then by herds of gazelles; sometimes vultures or eagles would glide high in the heavens. I remember, too, a valley dotted with herds of black and white sheep, with its row of black tents and groups of horsemen, the whole scene strangely enlivened by the low barking of dogs and the bleating of yaks and sheep.

GEOGRAPHICAL BACKGROUND

In earlier times, Tibetan tribes were distributed to the east of the present-day borders of Tibet, as far as the provinces of Szechwan and Kansu, and probably even through Shensi to Honan. Even today, there are Tibetan tribes in Szechwan and Kansu that have been strongly influenced by Chinese culture; they have often adopted the Chinese language. In the course of the last hundred years, the boundary between Szechwan and Kansu on the one hand, and eastern Tibet (i.e., the present Chinese border provinces of Sikang and Tsinghai) on the other, has been shifted several times. The Chinese government was impelled to do this in Kansu because of the gradual advance of the Chinese towards the west and also because of difficult relations with the third element in the population of Kansu, the continuously restless Moslems. Although the latter have adopted the Chinese language, dress, and customs, they have by no means been assimilated by the Chinese but are consciously opposed to them. According to physical characteristics, they can be included among the Turkish peoples of Chinese Turkestan (Sinkiang). The Chinese and Moslem settlers have penetrated into Kansu wherever the Chinese farmer has found proper conditions, particularly loess soil, for the type of agriculture he has practiced since time immemorial. In places where the valley bottoms lend themselves to irrigation, the river valleys have become rich oases with fertile vegetable and fruit farms in the midst of dry, treeless mountains. However, the mountainous country can also feed the tough and industrious Chinese and Moslem farmers given peaceful political conditions and a settled administration. Naturally, these highlands (1,500 to 3,000 meters) cannot support as dense a population as the lower and warmer loess regions of central and eastern North China.

South of the loess country in Kansu, the boundary toward Szechwan is formed by the Min Shan, a mighty mountain range over 5,000 meters high, a part of the Kunlun system. Only unimportant branches of Chinese culture have penetrated into this region from the north, since the conditions necessary for Chinese agriculture are lacking. Neither the narrow valleys, formed by the corrosion of limestone, primary rock, and granite, nor the rolling uplands higher than 3,000 meters are suitable for the Chinese farmer. Sedentary Tibetans (or sedentary Fantzu, as we shall henceforth call them, following Kansu colloquial usage) live in the valleys and the lower parts of the highlands. Even though the summers are relatively short, crops of Tibetan barley (ch'ing-ku), peas, and rape are relatively good. Thus, the sedentary Fantzu are able to provide themselves and the nomad tribes living higher up with the indispensable barley flour. These sedentary Fantzu lead a life somewhat different from that of the Chinese farmer, since for them livestock is more important than field crops. The yak serves them as mount and beast of burden and gives milk and butter, making them less dependent on crops in bad seasons. This food also provides them with a priceless source of health and energy in the cold mountain climate.

One is struck by the landscape of the country as one travels from Lanchow south through the Ho-chou area (modern name Lin-hsia) to the famous Labrang monastery, situated in the mountains south of the loess region. One reaches the T'ao River valley from the Yellow River valley by traveling through a loess region inhabited mainly by Moslems and further through a sparsely settled granite range, the crest of which is not quite 3,000 meters high. South of the T'ao River is a deeply furrowed loess region, which reaches almost 3,000 meters. This is bounded on the other side by the Hsia River and is inhabited by Moslems. In the Hsia River valley the percentage of Chinese is larger, but Islam, partly by means of bloody insurrections that were difficult to suppress, has made increasing headway since the beginning of the twentieth century. This is probably the main reason that the Chinese government has shifted the boundary between Kansu and Tsinghai farther west.

If you travel from Ho-chou up the wide, fertile valley of the Hsia River, which runs between loess plateaus, you soon come to steep, wooded mountains which are set off sharply from the loess country. The river breaks through these mountains through a narrow gorge and leaves them behind at T'u-men Kuan. This is the present boundary between the district of Ho-chou and the recently demarcated district of Hsia-ho, which formerly belonged to the Tibetan province of Amdo. This district boundary is, in fact, the dividing line between loess country and mountain country, and has long formed an ethnic boundary between Chinese and Tibetans. The narrows at T'u-men Kuan are closed off by an old wall, which may have been the chief line of defense for the Chinese against an enemy breaking through from the mountains. When I passed through in August, 1936, this barrier was occupied by Moslem soldiers, who intended to defend it against Mao Tse-tung's army. However, the Communists did not advance through the valley of the Hsia River but proceeded east to Kansu, since they were not

5

equipped for the march through the Tibetan highlands to Sinkiang. They would have found the Moslems tough opponents, prepared to resist them with determination, even though armed almost exclusively with spears decorated with red tassels.

Beyond T'u-men Kuan, the Chinese and Moslems have settled only in the principal valleys and even there almost exclusively as traders in small settlements along the caravan roads. They supply passing travelers and caravan drivers with food and shelter, sell sundries to the Tibetan country people, and buy local farm products. The region beyond T'u-men Kuan is settled mainly by Tibetans, who have preserved their culture relatively intact. A few kilometers up the valley one comes to the first Tibetan chorten and directly thereafter to the first lamasery. After a two-day journey from T'u-men Kuan, one reaches Labrang, situated at an altitude of 2,950 meters, near the place where the Hsia River, which rises in the rolling highlands farther south, begins to gnaw its way into the mountains.

The famous monastery of Labrang is a most important cultural and political center. It was founded in the eighteenth century during the reign of Ch'ien Lung, who was interested in furthering Lamaistic religion. Labrang is now an important monastery town with many magnificent temples and countless courts for the lamas. There are said to be around three thousand lamas and "living Buddhas" residing here. About 1 kilometer down the valley from Labrang, there is a small market town inhabited mainly by Moslems. Nine years ago the Chinese government made this the district capital of Hsia-ho. A detailed description of Labrang is given by Li An-che.[5] The Tibetans who live near Labrang are farmers, who grow Tibetan barley in the valleys of the Hsia River and its tributaries. If conditions are favorable, they also plant wheat, as well as oats, broad beans, rape, and flax. They raise yaks, sheep, goats, horses, and swine.

Somewhat south of Labrang begins the high Tibetan steppe. Its southern boundary toward Sikang and Szechwan is formed by the Min Shan. West of Labrang are the highlands of Tsinghai province. Although the timber line is at about 3,000 meters, the regions above it are farmed. In the treeless, flat, trough-shaped valleys between 3,000 and 3,500 meters, one finds small villages of sedentary Tibetans everywhere. Here they grow Tibetan barley and oats, often both in the same field, as well as rape. With increasing altitude, cultivation gradually lessens and from about 3,500 meters upward, one finds grassland inhabited only by livestock farmers.[6]

---

5. Li An-che, "A Lamasery in Outline," Journal of the West China Border Research Society, XIV, Series A (1942), 35-68.

6. Ekvall, op. cit., p. 29.

Although the Tibetans living here are under Chinese administration, they are not dependent on the Chinese and not particularly influenced by Chinese culture. They are divided into individual tribes, one of which (the Mewu Fantzu) will be described more closely in the following account. The territory of the Mewu Fantzu lies south of the large lamasery of Heh-tso and east of the old part of Taochow (Lin-t'an).[7] The tribe of the Mewu Fantzu consists of sedentary as well as nomad Tibetans.

After I had lived in Labrang and Heh-tso for some time, I visited two monasteries belonging to the Mewu tribe, the Old and the New Mewu monasteries (Mewu Chiu-szu and Mewu Hsin-szu). Then I pitched my tent 18 or 20 kilometers south of the latter monastery, in a shallow valley at a height of about 3,950 meters. On the slope of this valley stood twenty-three black Tibetan tents in a long row. I had good introductions from the New Mewu monastery, and since I had engaged a Chinese interpreter who had lived many years as a trader among the Tibetans,[8] I soon gained some-what closer contact with the local inhabitants.

PHYSICAL CHARACTERISTICS OF THE MEWU FANTZU

In physical features the Mewu Fantzu are by no means uniform; on the contrary, one is struck by the diversity of types. The men are medium to tall in height, measuring between 160 and 180 centimeters; the women are, on the average, about 20 centimeters shorter. The skin of the exposed parts of their bodies is dark brown; their hair is deep black. They have little armpit or facial hair. They do not always have pronounced epicanthic folds. Some of these Tibetans with their relatively long faces, slightly slanting eyes, somewhat prominent cheekbones, and long, flat-to-concave noses, cannot be distinguished from typical northern Chinese. Others, with rounder, flatter faces, more prominent cheekbones, concave noses, and slanting eyes with very pronounced epicanthic folds, look more like Mongols. Still others, with squarer faces, prominent cheekbones, and more

---

7. A good illustration of Heh-tso lamasery is given in Tafel, op. cit., Vol. II, Plate LXVII, facing p. 289.

8. Concerning the position of these traders in the social life of the Tibetan nomads, see Ekvall, op. cit., pp. 48 ff.

9. For a large selection of illustrations of ethnic types, see Hermanns, op. cit. According to Ekvall, op. cit., p. 9, the Fantzu of this region have "all the characteristics of a mongrel physical type."

prominent and rather narrow upper jaws, sometimes remind one of the Japanese. However, one also sees Tibetans who more closely resemble the Turkish inhabitants of Sinkiang, or even Europeans. They often have straight noses (especially those resembling Europeans), less prominent cheek-bones, and straight eyes with downward slanting eyebrows and without the epicanthic fold. In contrast, there are also persons (who, according to my observations, are more frequently found in Sikang) who have very prominent noses, reminding one of the aquiline-nosed North American Indians. There are others with narrow faces, delicate aquiline noses, and graceful bodies, resembling East Indians and gypsies. All this simply shows that the Fantzu are not a uniform race but the result of much racial intermixture.

The Tibetans are a strong people; I did not see a single asthenic type among the Mewu Fantzu. Apart from infectious diseases their health is good. The most frequent complaints of patients who came to see me were of rheumatism and stomach disorders. The latter often seemed to indicate chronic catarrh of the stomach and also stomach ulcers. There is a high incidence of conjunctivitis, which is probably often trachoma. Smallpox is prevalent among the acute, infectious diseases, and syphilis among the chronic ones. I did not observe any cases of tuberculosis, but there is leprosy, although it occurs infrequently despite the fact that lepers are not segregated. The ravages of syphilis are extreme, affecting the skin, mucous membranes, and bones.

Infant mortality is extraordinarily high. Most families have only one or two children, although women give birth to as many as ten. The reason for this may be the strange way babies are fed. People prefer to give their children yak milk rather than mother's milk because, they say, the latter makes them stupid. Although yak milk has a higher fat content than cow's milk, the children are given the boiled milk undiluted, often with butter and parched barley flour (tsamba) added.

CLOTHING AND ADORNMENT

Men's Dress. We shall touch only briefly on the dress of the Mewu Fantzu since it is like that of Tibetans in general.[10] The chief article of

---

10. Cf. Rockhill, op. cit., pp. 684 ff. Each tribe has its peculiar characteristics of dress, hair style, and adornment. Yet, despite the fact that Rockhill's illustrations and descriptions are not specifically of the Mewu Fantzu, they give one a good general idea of the tribal dress.

clothing is a large sheepskin coat. It has very long sleeves that extend far over the hands. The Fantzu prefer to put only their left arm into one sleeve, leaving the right arm and shoulder free. The nomad's coat usually has a neckband of leopard skin about 10 centimeters wide and a hem of black wool. Poor people omit the leopard-skin trimming or replace it with a border of pulu, a Tibetan woolen material. This is not made by the eastern Tibetans themselves but is imported from the highlands of central Tibet. The leopard-skin trimming is obtained ready-made from Chinese traders; the grassland itself does not supply enough skins for this purpose. Most of the skins come from the forest region of the Min Shan, where the Chinese traders obtain them from the local Fantzu. Ordinarily, and especially in summer, the Fantzu wear extremely dirty coats. During the warm season, they prefer worn pelts which have shorter hair than new ones. In winter and on festive occasions, they sometimes also wear a jacket under the coat. This may be of silk, pulu, or simple Chinese cotton, depending on the wealth of the wearer. This jacket is cut in the old Chinese style, with a placket trimmed with a bright-colored band about 3 centimeters wide. It has a high, stiff collar with a different colored cloth on each side, i.e., red inside and green outside. The color combination of the jacket (collar and bottom hem) can vary a great deal.

In former times, no trousers were worn in summer, but gradually the men are becoming accustomed to Chinese pants made of thin, dark-blue cotton. In winter they wear trousers of sheepskin, or only leggings, just like the northern Chinese. The fleece is worn against the bare skin; they wear no drawers. In winter and on festive occasions, a coat of pulu or silk (Chinese: tuan, satin) is worn over the sheepskin coat. The color of the former varies; it may be purple, blue, red, green, or black, but never white. The lower part of this coat is sewn with several bright-colored silk strips of various colors to give the impression of many coats, one on top of another. In rainy weather, coats of white wool with long sleeves are worn and, less frequently, capes of the same material. The woolen coat, like the sheepskin one, is simply tied together over the hips, never buttoned. Ordinarily, a coarse rope of braided yak hair is used for this purpose, but festive garb requires a red sash of Szechwan silk. All articles of clothing are made by the men, never by the women. The men also make their own Chinese trousers. Boys' clothing is the same as the men's.

The boots have a leather foot part and a leg made of pulu, or coarse wool.[11] The foot part is often simply a piece of soft yak leather cut to size

---

11. Ibid., Plate 2.

9

and then turned up on all sides, very much like the Indian moccasin or the opanke of the Balkan peoples. Into the foot part is set the leg shaft which reaches to the knees. The favorite material is red Russian leather imported by the Chinese from Kalgan, or bright-colored pulu cloth with a pattern in the form of a cross.

Many different kinds of headgear are worn.[12] The most popular is a round fur cap with a cloth tassel, usually red. The Fantzu prefer fox fur; however, lambskin caps are cheaper. For the latter, the fleece of a month-old lamb is used. This cap is indispensable for festive dress. In summer, it is often replaced by headgear consisting of a strip of gaily colored pulu cloth, usually with blue and yellow stripes. Felt hats are also worn, either a simple conical-shaped hat without a brim, made of thick, soft, un-bleached felt, or one of stiff felt in the form of a truncated cone, with a wide, flat brim.

Women's Dress. Women's dress is even less influenced by the Chi-nese than that of the men. In summer, it usually consists of a sheepskin coat; in winter, another coat is worn over this. The sheepskin coat is cut like that of the men and is also held together above the hips by a coarse belt. In summer, the women like to work with the upper part of their body free, so they slip out of the coat and let it hang down over the cord. The women's sheepskin coat differs from the men's in that it has a cloth neck-band, never a leopard-skin trimming. On the other hand, the lower hem of a woman's coat is trimmed with a wide, bright-colored band of cotton, or, in the case of a wealthy woman, of silk. The women do not wear trousers. When it rains, they wear woolen cloaks or, more often, woolen capes with only one opening, like the South American ponchos. The capes often have a pointed hood. In summer, women wear coats with short hair; in the winter, newer ones with long hair and over them a pulu coat. Festive dress does not differ from everyday garb, except that the clothes are new, and a colored coat of cloth is worn over the sheepskin coat.

At work and around the house, the women go barefoot in summer. The rest of the time, they wear the same kind of boots as the men. Only wealthy women are seen wearing Chinese shoes on festive occasions. The women do not wear pulu caps. In rainy weather, they wear the same soft felt hats that the men do when they go out to the pastures. A stiff felt hat is part of the festive garb of the women. It has the same truncated-cone shape as that of the men, but the cone is smaller in diameter and thus looks

---

12. Ibid., Plate 4.

more elegant. On top it has a copper ornament and a silk tassel,[13] which are bought from the Chinese.

Hair Style. The Fantzu wear the hair short; it is only at the top that some men still wear a small, thin braid that looks like a rattail. Their method of cutting hair is still very primitive. They find an old sickle which is no longer good for cutting grass and sharpen it on suitable field stones. Oddly enough, the Fantzu cut their hair from the top down, in contrast to the Chinese. Only the sorcerers (bömbu) wear long hair, which they wrap in a kerchief. Like the Chinese, they pluck out their beards with brass tweezers, which they carry on their rosaries or on a chain around their necks. Only lamas occasionally wear beards.

The women have a very complicated coiffure. At six or seven, little girls have their hair dressed for the first time. The hairdo consists of three rather thick braids that hang down from a part, and many smaller, thin braids on the sides, held together above the ears with a special ornament.[14] The coiffure of the women is the same, except that they wear many more braids that hang far down and are held together with a complicated ornament. Besides two center braids, the women wear 80 to 100 thin braids on either side. These braids must reach to the knees. Since a woman's hair is not long or thick enough for this type of coiffure, she buys false braids from Chinese traders.

Personal Hygiene. The Tibetans do not know much about caring for their bodies. They do not wash, and their bodies are covered with a black layer of dirt. Since they do not wash their sheepskin coats, conditions are ideal for the propagation of body lice. The Fantzu wash only the mouth, face, and hands with cold water. They do not use a wash basin for this but take a mouthful of water from a pottery jug, rinse out the mouth, and then spit the water into the hands, using it to wash face and hands. After washing, they rub butter on their faces. Also, if they have remnants of butter on their fingers after eating, they rub it on their faces. This gives them protection against the strong mountain sun.

Jewelry and Weapons. Both men and women lay more stress on ornamentation than on personal hygiene. The men wear one earring,[15] either on the right or the left ear. It is made of silver and usually set with a large red coral. The nomads also occasionally wear a large, ring-shaped ornament of silver set with corals above one ear. This is not, however, characteristic

---

13. Hermanns, op. cit., pp. 33-34.

14. A similar ornament of another nomad tribe is shown in Hermanns, op. cit., Illustration 51.

15. Rockhill, op. cit., Plate 6.

11

of their costume but belongs to that of the sedentary Fantzu living farther
south in the Labrang region. Less frequently, men wear simple silver rings.
A rosary is usually worn around the neck as a necklace. It is made of thick
black disks of fragrant wood or of small wooden beads which are simpler and
cheaper. Sometimes they wear the rosary at the belt or on the rope around
the hips.[16] The black necklace is called tsä-nga (Chinese: su-chu). Hanging on this chain is either a round disk resembling a Chinese chess figure or
a large, round amber or lacquer ball. On their thin rosaries they wear a
square or circular silver box containing some kind of sacred relic, mostly
pieces of cloth, amulets, and often a Buddha picture, usually that of the
Dalai Lama or the Panchen Lama.[17] The front of the box is always decorated with a coral in the center. The length of the sides and the diameter
of this small amulet box may vary a great deal, but they average 6 to 9
centimeters and 4 to 6 centimeters respectively. It is 1 to 2 centimeters
deep.

Apart from these ornaments, however, the men set great store by the
decoration of their weapons. They always carry their weapons with them
when they go any distance from their tents, even in times of peace. These
consist of a rifle, a sword, and a dagger. Until recently, old-fashioned
rifles were generally used, with the customary fork and a stock that often
had a beautiful silver mounting.[18] These old-fashioned guns are still made
in Ho-chou. Within the last four years, however, many comparatively
modern rifles have been sold to the Fantzu by Chinese army deserters. Even
these modern weapons often have forks which are made chiefly in Labrang.

Their swords are about 1 meter long.[19] They are not worn on a sword
belt but are stuck through the belt in front so that they rest almost horizontally. The haft and scabbard are usually richly decorated with silver mountings set with corals. A knife about 30 centimeters long hangs at the side,
its handle and sheath consisting of brass or silver.

The women wear large, silver ear pendants, richly set with corals and
turquoises. At the age of seven or eight, little girls get their first earrings,
mostly of simple brass. Finger rings of silver or copper, also set with corals
and turquoises, are worn on the left hand.[20] Neck rings and necklaces are
not worn. Special emphasis is put on hair ornaments. When the young girls
get their first hairdo, the side braids are held together by a special ornament,

---

16. Ibid., Plates 35, 36.
17. Ibid., Plate 5.
18. Ibid., Plate 23.
19. Ibid., Plate 22.
20. Ibid., Plate 5, Figure 12.

as we have mentioned. This is made of cloth which the women themselves sew and trim with corals.[21]

The women carry an important tool which has at the same time developed into an ornament. It is an anchor-shaped double hook of brass, known in Tibetan as sao-sou (Chinese: nai-kou, milking hook).[22] It is usually set with a few corals. It is always worn at the belt and is used to hold the pail while milking. Sometimes the belt is also ornamented with strips of red cloth and tassels.

The Tibetans spend a great deal of money, relatively speaking, on their ornaments. I quote the following prices: silver earrings for a man, 2 to 3 yuan;[23] corals for these, 2 to 3 yuan; finger rings, . 50 yuan, or 50 fen. The heavy rosaries of fragrant wood with pendant cost from four to several hundred yuan; the thin ones, 1 to 3 yuan. The small silver boxes attached to the rosaries and worn on the chest cost 10 to 15 yuan, and an additional 1 to 2 yuan is spent on the coral in the center. Simple old-fashioned rifles cost only 10 yuan, but the Fantzu pay 200 or 300 yuan for good modern ones. Swords cost from 2 to 40 yuan, depending on the decoration and the amount of silver and coral used. The women's earrings cost from 4 to 15 yuan, while the brass earrings for young girls cost no more than 1 yuan. The girls' hair ornaments cost . 50 yuan; those of the women 10 to 100 yuan, depending on the amount of coral and whether they are made of silver or brass. Women's silver rings, without corals or stones, cost 1 or 2 yuan. The brass mounting on a hat costs 20 to 30 fen. The milking hook costs 2 to 10 yuan, according to its coral decoration. The women folk of the sedentary Fantzu wear much more expensive ornaments, which may cost several hundred yuan.

None of these ornaments is made by the Tibetans, but by the Chinese, who now frequently sell very cheap and inferior ornaments of brass. Valuable and artistic ornaments, however, come from central Tibet and Sikang. Genuine corals and semiprecious stones (turquoise and malachite) are likewise imported from central Tibet, whereas imitation coral is imported from China.

---

21. A description of women's hair styles is found in Rockhill, op. cit., p. 690.

22. Illustrated in K. Futterer, Durch Asien (Through Asia) ("Geographische Charakter-Bilder" [Geographical Sketches], Vol. I [Berlin: Dietrich Reimer, 1901]), p. 341.

23. At the time of my visit, the Chinese dollar, or yuan, was the equivalent of 50 cents in American currency; Chinese paper money, which even at the time had a considerably lower rate of exchange, was not accepted by the nomads.

NOMAD COMMUNITIES

The nomadic Mewu Fantzu are grouped together in separate tent communities, but these are very loose associations. Such a tent camp consists of from four to forty tents, the average being twenty to twenty-five.

The nomads change their place of residence three times a year. They move to the first tent camp in the third Chinese month and remain there until the sixth. From then to the eighth Chinese month, they occupy the second camp. Thereafter, they descend to lower altitudes and stay there until the third or the fourth Chinese month. During this time, they do not live in tents but in simple mud huts grouped together in smaller or larger units. Each family returns to the same house every year.

The individual tent communities do not always consist of the same families; the tribal chief (Chinese: t'ou-mu) determines which tent community a family must join.

The winter pasture is always the same for each family. Near the winter house each family plants oats, which they cut green and use for fodder during the winter. There is enough land so that everyone can plant as much oats as he needs for his cattle. The two summer pastures are not always the same, a particular pasture being used only once every two years. Thus one family lives in five different pastures in the course of two years, one winter pasture and two summer pastures per year. The distances between the pasture areas of a tent community are never very great. For example, the following were the distances between the pasture areas of the community in which I lived: winter camp to first summer camp, over 20 li; first summer camp to second summer camp, about 20 li; second summer camp to winter camp, 40 to 50 li.[24]

The tents of a community are, as a rule, pitched on the slope of a shallow valley. They are in long rows at irregular distances (20 to 200 meters) from each other so that the entire settlement can be 2 to 4 kilometers long. It is usually too damp to pitch a tent on the valley floor. The choice of site for a tent camp is primarily determined by water conditions.

DWELLINGS

The tents are not all the same size.[25] Smaller tents are about 4 by 8 meters, larger ones about 5 by 15 meters. The cloth of the tent is a very

---

24. The Chinese li is about six hundred meters.

25. Illustrations in Futterer, op. cit., pp. 336, 342; detailed

14

coarse, blackish-brown material woven of yak hair. It is made by either the nomad women or the women of the sedentary Fantzu. The cost of the material for the entire tent averages about 50 yuan. The floor of the tent is simply tamped earth. The tent itself is made up of a wall and a roof. The wall, about 1.3 meters high, is a width of cloth which encloses the tent and is fastened on stakes of the proper height. The roof is made of widths of cloth sewn together, stretched horizontally, and fastened at a height of 1.8 meters to four poles. These poles form a rectangle within the wall, the sides of the rectangle being about 1 meter from the wall. Cloth strips about 1.5 meters wide are sewn to the sides of the tent roof. These are fastened to shorter poles which, in front, are about 1.8 meters, on the sides and in the rear, about 1 meter high. The strips are attached outside the tent walls in such a way that they slant outward. Thus, the entire space enclosed by the tent wall is covered. Around the tent a large number of longer and shorter poles and stakes are driven into the ground in order to stretch the large, horizontal middle section of the tent roof and the slanting sides. These posts are fastened to the cloth of the roof with strong ropes made of yak hair. The horizontal roof consists of two symmetrical halves which converge in a line at the center of the two longitudinal sides. These halves can be pulled apart slightly to permit smoke from the fireplace below to escape.

The fireplace is always in the exact center of the tent and divides it into two equal halves. It consists of a very primitive, rectangular hearth made of mud about .5 meters high. On the left side of the hearth, as seen from the entrance, there are three fire holes. There are three corresponding holes on top, into which the cooking pots are set. The hearth does not extend the whole breadth of the tent, and towards the rear it stops at the place where the fuel (dried yak dung) is stored. In front of the hearth is the entrance to the tent, separated from the hearth by a screen, which is simply a piece of cloth about 2 meters wide stretched between two poles. Thus, when one enters the tent, one does not come directly into the main room but into a sort of anteroom formed by the cloth screen in front of the hearth; also one enters either the left or the right half of the tent, since the two halves are sharply separated by the hearth and the adjacent fuel storage area.

The side of the tent to the right of the entrance is used only by the men, that to the left by the women. It is strictly forbidden to step across the hearth or the place where the fuel is stored. It is also considered very

_____

descriptions in Hermanns, op. cit., p. 43; and Ekvall, op. cit., pp. 74-75.

impolite to step over a person lying on the tent floor. A stranger may under no circumstances enter the side reserved for the opposite sex. The residents of the tent may set foot in the forbidden half only if they are alone in the tent and need to fetch something from the other side. The women, however, may not sit down in the right half. The husband goes over to the left side to sleep.

In the section to the right, the hearth is connected to a very primitive type of k'ang (two short tubular passages in which a fire is kindled, connected with the hearth so that the fire gets a proper draft).[26]

The household furnishings are placed along the wall where the roof slopes down and the tent is lower. Near the rear wall of the right side, next to the fuel storage area, is the family altar, a simple, rectangular wooden box about .5 meter high, 40 centimeters deep, and 1.5 meters long. On this altar stand bronze statues of the Buddha and small bowls of holy water. The rest of the space along the tent wall is chiefly filled with bags made of coarse yak hair in which are stored dried yak and sheep dung, saddle gear for horses and yaks, and skins. Rifles are often kept on a separate stand. Dried meat and yak maws, in which butter is stored, are hung from the ceiling. A section of the right side of the tent is sometimes provided with a couch made of boards not more than 20 centimeters high and covered with dogskins.

The women's section on the left contains the utensils needed in the dairy. These are chiefly three cylindrical wooden tubs 1 to 1.5 meters high and 75 centimeters in diameter, with staves held together by withes. One of these tubs, usually the smallest and the one nearest the rear wall, is used to store sour milk. In the center is the churn and nearest the front is a large milk tub. The churn is closed at the top and has a hole through which runs a long, heavy dasher. Suspended from the ceiling of the tent, above the milk tub, is a bag of coarse material through which the whey can be strained from the curds.

Near the tent there is driven into the ground a short stake to which the dog is tied. In front of many tents there are also one or two poles 3 meters in height, with lines from which prayer pennants hang. Very occasionally, there is a simple, round sheepfold made of boards and poles next to the tent.

----

26. The main room of a house in North China has a k'ang located near the outer wall opposite the door. It is a brick box from 60 to 70 centimeters high and hollow inside. It serves both as a couch and a stove, is equipped with drafts, and is fired through a hole in the outer wall.

The winter houses are very primitive. They are usually placed along the rear wall of a courtyard and enclosed by a mud wall 2 meters high. The only opening in the enclosure is a gate in the front wall. A large part of the yard is set off by a low wall and serves as a cattle pen. Opposite this, on the narrow side, is a stall for horses and yaks. It consists merely of a roof about 2 meters wide and is open toward the yard. The house itself contains two rooms about 2 meters high, with simple mud walls and a Tibetan-style flat roof formed of horizontal wooden beams laid side by side and covered with layers of earth. The two rooms are furnished with simple k'angs which are heated from the outside, as in China. Almost all the winter houses look very dilapidated. Next to the winter houses one sometimes sees large stacks of dried yak dung, resembling our haystacks.

DIVISION OF LABOR

The daily schedule and work of the tent nomads is very simple. They sleep surprisingly little. They get up at the crack of dawn and do not go to bed until two or three hours after dark. Only occasionally do they take a nap in the middle of the day. As soon as they get up, they milk their animals and drive them out to pasture.

The men work very little. Their favorite occupations are riding and paying calls, during which the main topics of conversation are pasture conditions and choice of pasture sites. When it has grown dark, they chat and drink tea.

Practically all the rest of the work falls on the women. They must milk, make butter, and dry curds. Cooking, however, takes little time in view of the simplicity of the Tibetan diet. The women also spin. The fleece is first washed in cold water, wrung out, and then dried on the meadow. For a distaff they use a short wooden stick from which they spin off thick yarn onto a simple spindle consisting of a wooden stick and a weight. The women take the wool they have spun to the sedentary Fantzu women, who can weave the cloth used to make bags for storing tsamba. The nomad women buy this cloth with money, butter, or wool. The cloth for their woolen coats and capes is woven by the Chinese in Ho-chou. The Chinese weaver gets about 1 fen per foot of cloth. The nomad women can weave only the coarse, yak-hair cloth from which tents are made. Both men and women twist coarse ropes of yak hair, which they use to pull the tent widths taut, for bridles, and for halters and hobbles. Other handiwork, such as knitting and embroidering, is not done by the nomad women. As mentioned previously, all articles of clothing are made by the men.

17

Gathering fuel is an important female occupation. They must collect yak and sheep dung, dry it, and stack it properly. This work is done
by the older women, never by the men. Nomad women do not go into
other regions to work as hired hands, as do the women of the sedentary
Fantzu. Year in and year out their whole time is taken up with caring for
the animals and the dairy.

The children are put to work tending the animals at an early age.
In addition, the girls must gather dung, but the boys do not help them with
this occupation. The girls start to milk the cows when they are twelve or
thirteen years old.

ANIMAL HUSBANDRY

Livestock raising is the sole means of subsistence for the Mewu Fantzu.
Their domestic animals are yaks, cattle, sheep, horses, and dogs. The
most important animal is the yak. The yaks of the Mewu region are generally pure black, occasionally black with white spots. There are horned
and hornless varieties. Lack of horns seems to be a recessive hereditary
characteristic. There are wealthy families who own more than 100 yaks,
but the average number is much less. The Fantzu in the tent colony where
I lived owned 700 yaks, an average of 35 per family. The highest number
of yaks per family was 70, the lowest 7. Sometimes poor people do not
own any yaks at all but merely rent them. A family of five needs more
than 10 milch yaks.

Not all families have bulls, but the owner of a bull does not receive
a breeding fee. A cow drops her first calf when she is two or three years
old. The gestation period of the yak is nine months. Most calves are born
in the third or fourth Chinese month, and in the seventh or eighth Chinese
month the cows are again bred. Good cows are allowed to grow very old;
they are killed only when they are seventeen or eighteen years old. A calf
is gradually weaned, but the amount of milk it gets is reduced very soon
after birth. When it is one or two months old, the calf gets a nose plug to
prevent it from sucking. The adult yak has a nose ring made of a bent
length of sturdy withe. Calves and young bulls are often driven to pasture
in pairs with their forelegs tied together so that they cannot stray.

Oxen are used as pack animals when they are three years old. At the
age of fifteen or sixteen, they are fattened and killed. Yaks graze all year
round; only when there is deep snow, which may happen in the twelfth and
first Chinese months, are they fed green oats. Yaks are never given any salt
and therefore always show a definite hunger for it. Milking is done exclusively by the women and girls. A yak cow will let herself be milked only

when her calf is tethered nearby. A very good milch cow gives a bucket of milk three times a day; an average cow gives two buckets a day, a bucket holding an average of 2.5 liters. Buckets are made and repaired by the Chinese of fine wood, first-class ones of cypress; withes are used as hoops.

Milk is drunk boiled or eaten when curdled. Most of it, however, is used to make butter. Casein is derived from the buttermilk and is filtered through a coarse bag, whereupon it is dried, stored in the form of coarse powder, and eaten. Whey is fed to the dogs. Butter is stored in sheep or yak maws, often for a long time, as much as ten years. This old butter, which gets very rancid, is used chiefly at the lamaseries to feed guests during festivals or to make Buddha images. Surplus butter is sent to the temple in which the son of the family is a lama (see section on religion). Lamas often come to the tents and ask for butter, which is always given to them willingly. The price for old and new butter is the same. It amounts to 50 fen per chin.[27] At home, as well as in the temple, butter is clarified in order to purify it. The resulting lard is used only as fuel for altar lamps.

The long yak hair from the animal's belly, back, and legs is plucked once a year in the fifth or sixth Chinese month. This is done by tying down the yak, winding the hair around a stick of wood, and pulling it out in tufts. Yak hair is used to make tent cloth and ropes.

A four-year-old milch cow costs 15 to 20 yuan, an old ox ready to be killed, 12 to 13 yuan. Calves are not sold. Yaks are killed mostly in the eighth and ninth Chinese month. Some of the fresh meat is eaten, but most of it is hung up to dry. The dried meat is either hung in the tent or packed in leather. In this packed state it is often given to a temple for safekeeping. A yak skin costs from 1 to 4 yuan; a good yak tail costs 10 fen, a white one 20 or 30 fen. Yak horns are used as snuff containers, occasionally as drinking horns. They also serve as milk bottles for babies.

Beef cattle are raised only by the sedentary Fantzu, not by the tent nomads. The tent nomads buy individual bulls for breeding because they like very much to crossbreed beef cattle and yaks. A cross between a bull and a yak cow (Chinese: p'ien-niu) is particularly valued. The p'ien-niu grows larger than a yak and has somewhat shorter and curlier hair. Its tail is thick and bushy but, unlike that of the yak, it is clearly defined at the root. It has larger horns than the yak. The p'ien-niu lives longer than the yak, reaching an age of twenty years or more. P'ien-niu bulls are almost always castrated and used as pack oxen. The p'ien-niu is valued because of its greater strength, longer life, and better milk production; it also

_____

27. The chin or Chinese pound equals about 605 grams.

withstands the warmer climate of lower altitudes better than the yak. The p'ien-niu has an importance to the yak breeder analogous to the importance of the mule to the horse breeder.

The p'ien-niu cow drops her first calf after three or four years. The price of a milch cow fluctuates between 40 and 50 yuan and is thus twice as high as that of a yak cow. A yak maw full of butter is the annual rent for a good p'ien-niu. (A maw contains about 18 chin.)

The cross between a yak bull and a beef cow is called szu-p'ien-niu in Chinese. It is not considered as valuable as the p'ien-niu, although it also lives to be some twenty years old. The szu-p'ien-niu has a bushy tail, smaller horns, and weaker legs than the p'ien-niu. It costs 30 to 40 yuan. The cross between a yak bull and a p'ien-niu cow (chia-p'ien-niu) is valued even less. Its hide is similar to that of beef cattle, but it is a larger animal. This crossbreed lives to be only ten years old. It costs about 30 yuan. The crossbreed between a bull and a p'ien-niu cow is called a ga-ba. It lives to be no more than seven or eight years old. A ga-ba calf is usually slaughtered immediately, and its mother is then used for milking.

Sheep are second in importance to yaks among the domestic animals.[28] One family seldom owns more than 700 sheep; there are also families that have no sheep at all. In the community of twenty tents where I lived, there were seven families that had no sheep. The total number of sheep in this community was more than 9,000, an average of 700 per herd owner. Sheep are not leased. One figures 40 to 50 ewes to 1 ram. Sheep drop their first young at two years; thereafter, the ewe drops only 1 lamb per season. A good ewe is allowed to die a natural death; otherwise, sheep are killed when they are two or three years old. Wethers are killed at three or four years. A good sheep costs from 3 to 3.5 yuan, a fat wether 9 yuan.

Like the yaks, the sheep are driven to pasture early in the morning and back to the tents at night. Some herd owners have simple, circular sheepfolds made of wooden beams next to their tents into which they drive their sheep at night.

The sheep are sheared once a year in the fourth or fifth Chinese month. Neighbors help each other at this task. It takes an average of two days to shear the herd of one family. A wether gives 1 chin of wool annually, a ewe .5 chin, a chin costing 20 to 50 fen. At the time of my visit, the demand for wool was so great that the highest price was paid. A sheepskin costs from 60 fen to 1 yuan. However, the skin of an unborn lamb costs from 2 to 4 yuan. A sheep gut is sold for 20 to 30 fen; in Heh-tso, the nearest large town, the price rises to 40 fen when it is resold.

---

28. Cf. Hermanns, op. cit., p. 87.

More mutton than yak meat is eaten. Lambs are eaten only if they have died of some disease. Fantzu do not drink sheep milk, but they use it to make butter if they do not have enough yak milk.

Sheep often suffer from paralysis of both forelegs, and many die of this disease. Mortality among sheep is highest in the first and second Chinese month, especially if there has been much snow during the winter; at that time many sheep die of starvation. If a family loses all of its animals, other families help by giving it sheep. The tent nomads do not usually keep goats, but the sedentary Fantzu often do, and they also drink goats' milk.

Every family has at least one horse. The Mewu Fantzu have a small breed of horses that measures 130 centimeters at the withers. These Tibetan ponies are somewhat smaller and lighter than Mongolian ponies, or those from the provinces of Tsinghai and Kansu. They are closer to the tarpan (Equus gmelini) than to the Przhevalski type.[29] These horses have a great deal of endurance and are especially adapted for use in mountainous terrain. They have hard hoofs, which are not shod in the steppes. Good stallions are selected for breeding; all others are castrated at four years. These horses, which are broken at three years of age, live an average of ten years. The average price of a riding horse is 40 to 50 yuan, the highest price being 100 yuan. No horses are imported, and horse traders come from Taochow and Heh-tso to buy horses from the Mewu Fantzu. Mules are not used by the tent nomads; they cannot stand the high altitude.

The simple leather bridles with brass mountings are made and sold by the Chinese, as are the iron bits and stirrups of iron or brass. The Mewu Fantzu use saddles with wooden frames which are made by the sedentary Tebu Fantzu on the northern slopes of the Min Shan and sold to the nomads.[30] These frames are put together by nomad saddlers. The frame is put on a thick felt pad which serves as a saddle cushion and is covered with gaily patterned pulu. The saddle is cushioned somewhat and is covered with leather; often it is decorated with brass mountings.

Each tent has at least one or two dogs. One of them is kept on a chain fastened to a stake; the other is allowed to run loose. In the winter, a hole is dug for the chained dog so that he can protect himself from the cold. Dogs get to be about 80 centimeters tall and have very shaggy coats, especially in winter, of black, yellowish-brown, or yellowish-gray color. They are

---

29. Ibid., pp. 164 ff.

30. Cf. Rockhill, op. cit., pp. 716 f. Wooden frames are used as pack-saddles for yaks and p'ien-niu, as they are in China. Ibid., Plate 26.

very alert and bark at the slightest provocation. Often every dog in the camp will bark for hours, especially at night, when they catch the scent of some beast of prey. It is very difficult to approach a tent because of these dogs. One must always have one's pockets and hands full of stones to defend oneself against them. One can safely approach a tent only when its occupants hold back the unleashed dogs. Riders usually carry a stick 60 or 70 centimeters long to which is fastened a leather whip about 1 meter long with an angular iron tip. When they pass or stop at a tent, they twirl it about to protect their horses from the dogs. You often see horses with large scars on their hind shanks from dogbites; the horses are particularly afraid of dogs and often become restless. even when they hear a dog bark far away. The dogs are fed tsamba and whey, and sometimes meat scraps. A good watchdog costs about as much as a yak, a less desirable one as much as a sheep. The dogs are allowed to grow old and die a natural death. A good dogskin, which is preferred as a couch cover, may sometimes cost only 2 yuan but usually costs 10 yuan or more.

AGRICULTURE AND HUNTING

The only field crop which the tent nomads plant is oats; each family sows some next to its winter dwelling. The crop is sown in the fifth Chinese month and is cut green in the ninth or tenth. It is used as winter fodder for horses and, less frequently, as yak fodder. All the oat fields belong to the tribal chief and are apportioned by him; rent for them, usually in the form of butter, is paid him by each family. The oat fields are plowed by oxen shortly before sowing time. The amount of oats planted depends on the size of the family and its wealth in livestock and ranges from 1 to 4 t'ien. A t'ien (a day's work) is usually 15 mou (about 1 hectare). The tent nomads utilize very few wild plants. From the fifth to the eighth Chinese month, they gather many mushrooms on the alpine meadows. They also gather chüo-ma, the edible tubers of Potentilla anserina, which are cooked like vegetables, and the roots used to make incense sticks. Wood is used only for tent stakes, poles for prayer pennants, and sheeppens. Pine, which is bought from the sedentary Fantzu, is generally used for these purposes.

Hunting is not an important occupation because the Mewu Fantzu are relatively strict Buddhists. They have no hunting dogs. It is only by chance that an animal which may be valuable in one way or another is killed; now and then a gazelle hunt is arranged. Trapping is not practiced. The Mewu Fantzu do hunt marmots, hares, gazelles (Gazella gutturosa Pall.), blue sheep (Pseudois najaur Hdgs.), musk deer, foxes, wildcats, lynxes, and

22

wolves. The latter are especially feared because they prey on the livestock; human beings are scarcely ever attacked by wolves. Birds are not
eaten and therefore are not hunted. Occasionally, a vulture is shot and its
wing bones are used to make flutes.

FOOD AND COOKING UTENSILS

Since the nomads are exclusively cattle raisers, they are restricted
primarily to an animal diet. (See section on taboos.) Their most important
food is butter. As we have said, they keep it for a long time, although most
people prefer fresh butter. They also eat dried casein in the form of a
coarsely ground powder (Tibetan: chü-ra) and fresh, sour, and boiled milk.
Whey is drunk only by poor people; usually it is fed to the dogs. All vegetable foods and condiments, with the exception of mushrooms and chüo-ma,
must be bought. The only important vegetable food is tsamba, with which
the nomads are always adequately supplied by either the neighboring sedentary Fantzu or the Chinese, who sell it to them by weight. It is stored in
bags of coarse woolen material. Wealthy people occasionally store a large
supply of tsamba, enough for two or three years, in a temple.

The ordinary meal consists of butter and tsamba, usually proportionally
more of the former. The Mewu Fantzu fill a wooden bowl with tea and add
a good lump of butter (about one heaping tablespoonful) which melts in the
hot tea.[31] As they drink the buttered tea, they try to blow aside as much as
possible of the butter floating on top, until a certain amount of tea and
butter remain in the bowl. Then they pour a suitable amount of tsamba into
the bowl and knead it into the remaining tea and butter with their fingers.
When they have shaped it into a ball, they eat it without adding any other
ingredients. Casein powder is also soaked in tea. Meat, whether yak or
sheep, is not eaten every day. The nomads eat the meat of animals which
have been killed or have died of some disease. (See section on the feeding
of infants.)

Sheep and yaks are not slaughtered but strangled. They are killed
in the eighth and ninth Chinese months, after they have been fattened on
summer pasture. As a rule, a yak is killed jointly by several families. Most
of the meat is dried, but some of it is eaten fresh. The latter is always
boiled, never roasted. Hunks of cooked meat are cut off with a knife and
eaten with the fingers. The intestines are stuffed with tsamba or Chinese

---

31. Ibid., Plate 14, Figure 3. Such a bowl is, on the average, 5 centimeters deep and has a diameter of 10 to 12 centimeters at the top.

bread (mo-mo) and eaten. The large intestine is generally used for this
purpose, since the nomads have found that they can profitably sell the
small intestine. Mo-mo is bought from Chinese bakers who live in the
settlements near the monasteries. Pork is eaten only at New Year's. For
this occasion wealthy families buy one or two pigs from the sedentary
Fantzu. Poorer people buy no more than one pig for which they pay in butter the following summer.

Besides pork which, according to Hermanns, is not generally eaten
by the Amdo nomads,[32] yak meat and mutton are also eaten at New Year's
and at feasts, along with butter, tsamba, pastry made of unparched barley
flour, and mo-mo, which is usually fried in rapeseed oil. The nomads
also buy noodles made of wheat or bean flour, carrots, and white cabbage
in Ho-chou. For feasts wealthy people prepare dumplings filled with garlic,
Chinese style. Rice is also occasionally served. It is prepared in various ways,
preferably boiled until it is soft, with sugar added.

Garlic and red pepper are the chief condiments along with hua-chiao
(Zanthoxylum piperitum D.C.). Salt comes from Tsinghai. Wine is purchased from the Chinese, who make it from Tibetan barley. It is not very
potent. Most Tibetans drink only on festive occasions, but now and then
one finds alcoholics. When drunk, the Fantzu often get very raucous and
crude; then they sing, shout, and brandish their swords. These drinking
bouts often end in a brawl and sometimes in manslaughter.

Most Tibetans do not smoke, since tobacco is very expensive. When
they do, they either buy pipes from the Chinese or make them of wood or
bone. They use a sheep tibia as do the northern Chinese in Shansi. Taking
snuff is much more common than smoking. The snuff, which contains no
tobacco, is made by the Mewu Fantzu from a mixture of tobacco ashes and
the finely pulverized ash that remains when sheep dung is burned, or else it
is bought from the Chinese in Ho-chou. Chinese snuff is made of wood ashes
mixed with various "medicines." Snuff is stored in yak horns or in snuff-
boxes.[33]

The nomads eat three meals a day. Breakfast is eaten rather late,
after the livestock have been milked and driven out to pasture. The midday
meal is eaten when the sun is at its height, the evening meal rather late,
after dark. The food, mainly tsamba and butter, is the same at all meals.
Guests are also served three meals. Men and women eat the same food but

---

32. Op. cit., p. 58. According to Ekvall, op. cit., p. 78, only the
nomads living at a great distance from the Chinese eat no pork.

33. Cf. Rockhill, op. cit., Plate 17, Figures 2-4.

are not permitted to eat together in the tent. The men eat in the right-hand section of the tent, the women in the left. The food must be handed from one section to the other around the hearth for it is considered very impolite to hand it over the hearth.[34]

Large brass kettles about 80 centimeters in diameter and 60 centimeters high are used for cooking. Most of them are made in Taochow, a large copper and brass center. A kettle of this type costs 10 to 20 yuan. The large, copper tea kettles are also made in Taochow, as well as the stands for the tea kettles and the tripods of brass or iron. The tsamba is kept in square boxes open at the top; bulkier provisions are kept in bags. Wooden bowls from Szechwan (Sung-p'an) are commonly used for tea and food; Chinese porcelain bowls are rarely used. Chinese from the Ho-chou region also supply cheap bowls made of birch. Large iron ladles are used in cooking. These must not be put into the mouth nor touch the edge of the bowl. Homemade wooden spoons are also used in cooking. Small table-spoons, mostly of birch, are imported from the sedentary Fantzu who live in the forested area (Sung-p'an, for example); from the Tebu Fantzu of the Cho-ni region; or from the Chinese.

The mud hearth has been described in the section on dwellings. Only sheep and yak dung are used for fuel, the sheep dung being used to kindle the fire. The dung is collected by the women, usually by the younger girls. Willow baskets are used to gather it. Afterwards it is carefully dried. A large basket full of dried yak dung, enough for two days of cooking, costs 4 fen. Matches are used occasionally, but flint and steel are still commonly employed.[35] The steel has a silver handle set with pearls. The fire is fanned with a simple sheepskin bellows to which a crude iron tube is attached.[36] The bellows has a conical shape and the iron tube is attached to the point. In fanning, the large opening at the base of the bag is rhythmically squeezed with the lower arm. The fire also serves to light the tent. Lamps, which consist of small, shallow copper or brass bowls about 6 centimeters in diameter, are used only for ritual purposes. Only carefully clarified lard is burned in them.

---

34. In order not to offend the spirit of the hearth. Cf. Hermanns, op. cit., p. 48.

35. Rockhill, op. cit., Plate 9, Figures 2-4.

36. Ibid., pp. 708 f.

HANDICRAFTS

One can hardly say that the tent nomads have any special craft. The women know how to spin wool but cannot weave. The only craft by which a woman can earn money is that of hairdressing. Only the men can sew, and they make all the clothing and shoes. They use Chinese cotton thread and crude needles imported from Szechwan. Tents are made mainly by lamas. The only men's craft besides tailoring is saddle making. However, men often earn money as pack drivers.

Basketry is not highly developed. The large willow baskets used for gathering yak dung are sometimes made at home but are generally imported from the neighboring sedentary Fantzu. Shallow baskets are used for storing special provisions, such as mushrooms, and these are obtained from the Tebu Fantzu.

INCOME AND TAXATION

The livestock of the nomads constitutes their entire wealth; they have practically no money. Wealth in livestock varies greatly between rich and poor. It often happens that a family or an entire tent community suddenly becomes impoverished if a great many animals starve after a heavy snowfall or die during an epidemic. If a family loses all its animals, friends and neighbors help it out. There is very little begging. One never sees beggars in the nomad settlements; a few may be seen around the monasteries, where they get a little tsamba on festive occasions or at burials.

Taxation is still very low: 50 fen to 1 yuan, according to the size of the family, paid annually to the tribal chief. The Chinese police collect it from him twice a year in the second and eighth Chinese month. No tax need be paid to the lamaseries, but each family must contribute food to the general temple festivals and to those temples where they have relatives among the lamas. Lamas also frequently come to the tent camps to collect butter for the lamaseries. This is always freely given.

TRADE AND TRAVEL

Trade is entirely in the hands of the Moslems and Chinese, chiefly the former. Many things are purchased with money; farther in the interior there is more barter. During the first years of the Chinese Republic, yuan came into use in place of unminted silver (tael).[37] In 1936, there was no

---

37. Smaller units of exchange are the ch'uan and copper coins. One

26

paper money among the Fantzu, but it will soon replace silver, which is being recalled by Chinese officials.

The nomads sell the Moslems and Chinese the following animals and animal products: sheep, horses, and yaks; sheep guts; horse and yak hides; horse and yak tails; skins of sheep, lambs, unborn lambs, dogs, foxes, marmots, and, more rarely, skins of goats, gazelles, and wolves. After New Year's, for which pigs are slaughtered, they also sell pig bristles. Finally, they sell musk, field mushrooms, chüo-ma, and a plant used in making incense candles.

The Chinese sell to the Fantzu: dress goods (silk and cotton), leopard skins for the men's coats, ornaments, weapons, kitchen utensils, especially cooking pots, needles, thread, matches, and bridles with bit and stirrups. Woodenware, especially saddles, eating bowls, and spoons, comes chiefly from the sedentary Fantzu who live in southern Kansu and northern Szechwan. Tsamba is also purchased from the sedentary Fantzu.

Bargaining is carried on very cautiously. The Tibetans do not come out with the price immediately; according to a custom also widespread in China, the parties clasp hands under their long sleeves, and the price demanded of the buyer is indicated by stretching out the fingers. They keep a dead-pan expression so that they will not betray their real feelings. Such a transaction in sign language is not necessarily carried on by the two parties alone; bystanders may act as go-betweens or lend support to one of the parties. They do this in sign language under their sleeves.

The Moslem and Chinese traders come to the tent camps of the Mewu Fantzu.[38] and the Fantzu also often go to the Chinese settlements adjacent to the temples on the caravan road from Ho-chou to Labrang, or to the nearest Chinese cities. An important trading station for the Mewu Fantzu is the Chinese-Moslem settlement near the large monastery of Heh-tso; somewhat farther away and less important is the monastery of Ka-chia Chiu-szu; a large trading center still farther away is the one next to the large temple city of Labrang. The more sizable Chinese cities visited by the Mewu Fantzu are Taochow, Ho-chou, and Ning-ho. In Taochow they buy metalware, such as copper and brass kettles. Yaks are used for carting. They bring wood from the sedentary Fantzu region to Ho-chou and Ning-ho and buy goods with the money they have earned.

---

yuan equals 11 1/2 ch'uan; 4 ch'uan equal 36 fen; one ch'uan equals 49 copper coins.

38. Cf. Ekvall, op. cit.

The nomads do not go beyond these cities to trade, but they do un-
dertake longer journeys to famous shrines. Most of them go once in their
lives to Kumbum and several times to Labrang. Occasionally, small groups
of nomads go on pilgrimages to the large sacred cities of central Tibet,
Lhasa and Shigatse. In the summer of 1936, all the Mewu Fantzu under-
took the two to three-day pilgrimage to Labrang in order to see the Panchen
Lama, the spiritual head of the Lamaists, who happened to be there at the
time. Occasionally, a nomad accompanies lamas and "living Buddhas"
on journeys into central Tibet.

EDUCATION AND LANGUAGE

Formal education is unknown among the nomads. Only the lamas
are educated and versed in purely scholastic Tibetan knowledge. The only
laymen who can read are those who once were lamas themselves but who,
for some reason, left the order. All contracts and agreements are verbal.
The language of the nomads is the northeastern Tibetan dialect of
the former Tibetan province of Amdo. Some nomads speak a little Chinese,
which they learn from Chinese and Moslem traders with whom they do business.

NUMBERS AND MEASUREMENTS

In counting and calculating they often use their rosaries; as yet they
do not use the Chinese abacus. If they have complicated transactions, they
seek help from a lama. They do not use special measuring rods. Cloth is
measured in squares, the side of a square being equal to the width of a cloth
strip. They do not use square measure to reckon the size of their pastures;
only hills, roads, and brooks are designated as boundaries. They measure
oat fields in terms of a day's work, that is, the surface which can be ploughed
in one day by one yak. The unit of weight is the Chinese chin (pound) containing 32 liang (ounces). They try to approximate the weight determined
by Chinese officials in Heh-tso. Simple Chinese hand scales with a stone
as a sliding weight are used. Dry measure, like the Chinese tou (bushel),
is not used because no products are traded in this way.

CALENDAR AND HOLIDAYS

The Mewu Fantzu have adopted the Chinese calendar,[39] but they do not buy Chinese calendar books; the scholarly lamas figure out the Chinese calendar for the people and post it on the temple gates so that everyone will know whether the month is long or short and on which days the twenty-four chieh-ch'i (the dates according to which weather predictions are made) occur. The Fantzu do not celebrate any Chinese holiday except New Year's. Not everybody knows when his birthday is or how old he is. They celebrate only the birthday of a "living Buddha," which coincides with the death date of his previous incarnation.

THE ARTS

The Mewu Fantzu layman not only has no formal education but also practices none of the visual arts. Architecture, painting, and sculpture are practiced exclusively by the lamas. Only laymen who were once lamas occasionally engage in an art such as painting. Although the nomads are very fond of ornaments, all of their jewelry, except that which comes from central Tibet, is made by Chinese and Moslems, albeit in strict Tibetan style.

The nomad culture does, however, include folk as well as religious music. Their only musical instrument is the flute, which is made of brass or of a vulture's wing bones and is played by both men and women. They usually play in the spring, during the second and third Chinese months. They play in their tents, in the fields, and while traveling. Special occasions for music-making are New Year's and family festivals, where there is much drinking and courting. They enjoy singing and do a great deal of it, particularly the young men and girls, without instrumental accompaniment. They have drinking songs, herding songs, love songs sung on the mountains, and a New Year's song. Once I also heard a monotonous work song sung by women who were washing fleece. Most songs are sung in alternating parts for boys and girls. The melodies are reminiscent of melancholy Russian folk tunes, sometimes of alpine yodels. I succeeded in jotting down the following songs which were sung in alternating parts in the mountains:

---

39. This is true of the Tibetans in general. Cf. L. Austine Waddell, The Buddhism of Tibet or Lamaism. (London: W. H. Allen & Co., Ltd., 1895), p. 451.

29

I. 1. Do not go away.
    2. When you return, I'll tell you something nice.

II. 1. When you look up, you see mountains, and beyond
        the mountains there is a river.
     2. Even though corals and pearls look like stones,
        they are as precious as gold and silver.
     3. Even though my friend is Chinese, he is of
        royal blood.

III. 1. The arrow is fitted into the bow; the needles are
         in the case; we can sew silk well with them.
      2. It is much better if I can meet my Chinese friend
         on the slope of the mountains, near the huts.
         (This means: it is easier for the Tibetan girl
         to have a rendezvous with a Chinese than to
         work in her tent camp.)

IV. 1. I shall now climb the mountain; tell me whether
        there is a fu-yeh ("living Buddha") there and
        whether he will bless me (touch me with his
        hand).
     2. I shall now climb down into the valley; is there
        peace there now so that I can do my trading?
     3. I shall visit my friends in the village; will the
        villagers think ill of me? Is my friend at home?

RELIGION

The religious situation of the Tibetans is similar to that of the Chinese, inasmuch as a highly developed religious system was superimposed upon an ancient, primitive folk religion, which nevertheless remained alive in the hearts of the people. Just as the vulgar form of Taoism developed essentially from Chinese popular religion, so the Bon religion developed from Tibetan folk religion. In China, Confucianism and the specifically Chinese form of Buddhism have been superimposed on the folk religion; in Tibet, Lamaism as the specifically Tibetan form of Buddhism has been superimposed.[40] However, the role of Buddhism in China cannot compare

---

40. Cf. Rockhill, op. cit., p. 730. "Primitive Lamaism may be

30

in importance with that of Lamaism in Tibetan religious life. The chief reason why Lamaism has not supplanted Tibetan folk religion entirely is probably that Lamaism is a very exclusive, priestly religion, in the ritual of which the layman scarcely participates. Folk religion, on the other hand, corresponds more closely to the needs of the layman and is indispensable to him. In Tibet, just as in China, there has been some merging of Buddhism in its strictest sense and folk religion. In both countries, Buddhism has taken over and more or less assimilated cults, rites, and ideas from folk religion and thus satisfied the religious needs of the people. The only difference has been that Lamaism, in spite of its exclusiveness, is much more intimately interwoven with the religious, social, and economic life of the people than is Chinese Buddhism. The majority of the Chinese people are connected only superficially with actual Buddhism; most of them have very little or no contact with it. On the other hand, the religious life of present-day Tibetans is unthinkable without Lamaism.

We cannot, of course, attempt to give even a cursory description of Lamaistic religion in the following pages. It was also impossible for me during my brief stay with the Mewu Fantzu to gain a thorough knowledge of their folk religion. I must, therefore, limit myself to the information which my Chinese interpreter, who displayed obvious interest in religious questions, gave me; the facts I gathered with his help from extensive conversations with the Mewu Fantzu; and the personal observations I made during my stay. I shall try to give the main characteristics of the religious life of the Tibetan layman, in this case the tent-dwelling, cattle-raising Mewu Fantzu nomad.

Conversations with Tibetans dealing with their personal affairs and especially with religious questions are, of course, difficult. The Tibetans are very suspicious of strangers. Being unaccustomed to the sight of foreigners and being quite used to thinking in terms of magic, they are unable to understand the stranger's interest in their religious ideas and customs, which they themselves in most cases do not think about but simply accept. They are only too ready to fear that the stranger might cause harm with the knowledge he is seeking to gain. I was always obliged to wait for suitable occasions when I could bring the conversation around to religious problems as casually as possible. I often had to change the subject when I noticed

---

defined as a priestly mixture of Shivaic mysticism, magic and Indo-Tibetan demonolatry overlaid by the thinnest veneer of Mahayana Buddhism....
(L. A. Waddell, Lamaism and its Sects, in Imp. and Asiatic Quarterly Review, VII, and his Buddhism of Tibet, p. 17.)"

that my questions seemed suspicious to the Fantzu and take up the thread at another time or with some other person. In many respects I might have been better informed and penetrated more deeply into the religious thinking of the nomads if I had questioned a lama, but in that case I would have got the description from the viewpoint of the lama and would not have learned what was most important to the religious life of the layman.

SPIRITS

Chinese and Tibetan folk religions are very closely related. In both cases religious thinking centers around a belief in spirits, nature demons, and the souls of the dead. The most important religious acts concern the propitiating of these omnipresent spirits and the warding off of the misfortune they might cause. The belief in spirits and the rituals accompanying it are, in both folk religions, combined with a very primitive belief in magic and many other superstitions.

The Mewu Fantzu distinguish between actual evil spirits (djäxe-dan or djir-dan), and the spirits of the dead, which correspond to the Chinese kuei (Tibetan: dźeo). The evil spirits cause sickness in man and beast, war, and sometimes loss of money, against which the sorcerer must intervene. Exorcists in China and the lamas in Tibet do the same thing.

The kuei can bring the same kind of misfortune. The spirits of those who have met violent death are feared the most. Headless spirits, which inspire a particularly great fear, are also believed to exist. There are, among the Tibetans as among the Chinese, people who believe they can see ghosts.

If a kuei brings on an illness, the victim is possessed by the kuei and the sorcerer must drive him out. Once driven out, the kuei prefers to station himself at a crossroads, provided the sorcerer has not been able to destroy him. Hence, people avoid crossroads, especially at night, preferring to make a detour. The souls of the dead which enter the body of an animal, according to the Buddhistic belief of the transmigration of souls, are also feared, especially if they have met violent death.

There is also a belief in nature demons, mountain spirits, earth spirits, and water spirits. Earth spirits are everywhere and correspond to the t'u-ti shen of the Chinese. The earth spirit is called sa-tja and, like the t'u-ti, has a wife. He lives in a valley, usually near sources of water. If one offends earth spirits, they can avenge themselves by bringing sickness. If someone is seized with violent internal pains, it is feared that the earth spirits have been offended. One can offend them by scratching up the earth, a belief strongly reminiscent of the Chinese conception regarding feng-shui (geomancy).

I did not hear anything about water spirits among the Mewu Fantzu, but in Labrang there is a sacred spring. Once, as I was riding by, I saw four lamas slowly encircle the spring, singing and beating drums, a ceremony which is performed when the weather is unfavorable, particularly when it is too wet or too dry. There is also a cult of tree spirits among the sedentary Mewu Fantzu, who live below the timber line.

We must distinguish mountain spirits from earth spirits in the narrower sense. In Tibet, as in China, there are mountains whose spirits or gods are the object of special veneration. The most notable among these is the Amne Machin, a little-known range in the northeastern reaches of Tibet. In the large lamasery of Heh-tso, which lies between Labrang and the territory of the Mewu Fantzu, a friendly lamasery artist made a beautiful picture for me of Amne Machin as a mounted male god, surrounded by numerous other gods. Unfortunately, the picture was lost in the chaos of war.

Mountain Spirits. The mountain spirits most venerated in the Mewu Fantzu area are the ami, who are thought to reside in the obo.[41] It took me a long time and required many conversations before I was able to understand the whole complex of ideas surrounding the obo and its spirit.

Every mountain on which there stands an obo (Tibetan: lăb-dză) is particularly sacred. The obo of the nomadic Mewu Fantzu consists of a wooden structure into which sacrificial wooden arrows are stuck annually so that it looks like a bundle or bouquet of arrows, often more than 2 meters high.[42] Twigs from bushes are also stuck into this bundle of arrows. The arrows vary in size and may be a meter or more long. Every Fantzu visits the obo at least once a year and takes with him a wooden arrow or the branch of a shrub as an offering. The chieftain has the privilege of giving an especially long arrow. Tufts of sheep wool and khadaks[43] are also stuck into the obo.

---

41. Cf. Rockhill, op. cit., pp. 734 f. "Obo" is a Mongol word.

42. Illustration in Tafel, op. cit., Vol. II, Plate LXIV, facing p. 264.

43. The khadak, a silk scarf, is very important in the religious and social life of the Tibetans. In its simplest form it is a strip of thin, light-blue silk, 1 meter long and about 30 centimeters wide. It is imported from the city of Ch'eng-tu in Szechwan. It is used as an offering to the obo and, in the Lamaistic religion, to an incarnation whose blessing one desires. A khadak is always an appropriate gift.

The ami who dwell in the obo are regarded as tutelary spirits of man and beast; they guard against sickness, cattle diseases, and other misfortunes, such as war. Among sedentary Fantzu they not only protect the animals but make the fields fertile as well. In war the ami are leaders and protect people against being wounded. Personal offerings are often made to the obo or the ami, especially when there is sickness in the family or when other misfortunes occur. For example, I observed four riders with two long wooden arrows wound with juniper branches visit the obo near my tent and deposit the arrows there. Oddly enough I was told that the ami can be very much disturbed by predatory animals, wildcats, and foxes.

Once a year, when a general obo festival is held, the largest number of arrows and khadaks are offered. In time the weather destroys many arrows so that the obo only gradually increases in size.

It seems that obos are built on mountains which have been sacred since ancient times. At any rate my interpreter Wang had never seen a new obo built. However, the Fantzu say that the obos in the northeastern part of the area are much older than those in the northwest.

Each obo has its own particular anniversary. In the territory of the Mewu Fantzu, there is a large one that outranks the others and is worshipped by nomadic as well as sedentary Fantzu. Its anniversary is the fourteenth day of the fifth Chinese month. There are two more in the uplands, which are revered by the nomads only, and, at a lower elevation, three obos of the sedentary Mewu Fantzu. The cult of the obo is a noteworthy example of the syncretism of folk religion and Lamaism: the ami, which is imagined as living in the obo and which is, without doubt, an original element of Tibetan folk belief, has a strange relationship to the incarnations, or "living Buddhas," of Lamaistic religion. There is an obo for every lamasery, erected on a promontory overlooking it. Its dominating position is analagous to the position of the Chinese pagoda in relation to the district seat. In the magical thinking of the Tibetan, the ami dwelling in the obo is related to an incarnation (fu-yeh or huo-fu) (see section on the incarnations); thus, there exists a mystical trinity—obo, incarnation, and its corresponding Buddha or bodhisattva of the Western Paradise. As a result, certain festivals are celebrated at the obo and at the lamasery on identical days of the year.

The day of the obo festival is also celebrated as the birthday of the incarnation. My interpreter, in trying to explain to me the relationship between obo and incarnation, once compared the obo with the p'ai-wei, a Chinese ancestral tablet, since the deceased incarnation is thought of as dwelling in the obo as well as in the Western Paradise.

On New Year's Day, the fourth day of the first Chinese month, a festival is held in the temple of the lamasery. On this occasion, fireworks are set off in honor of the deceased incarnations. At the same time, there is a festival at the obo to invoke the mountain spirit. On this occasion, butter, tea, a wether, and cypress wood are offered. A piece of meat from each of the four legs, the breast, the ears, and the lower jaw are burned with the cypress wood to indicate that in reality the entire animal has been sacrificed. This offering is made to safeguard man and beast and to protect the country from war. Thus, Lamaistic religious practices are here combined with animal sacrifice and stand in sharp contrast to actual Buddhism.[44] It is also characteristic of the syncretism of folk religion and lamaism that sorcerers as well as lamas may offer sacrifice at the obo.

Household Spirits. Whereas the ami are tutelary spirits of the entire tribe, each family also venerates special guardian spirits within its tent. These might be compared to the ancient Roman lares familiares. My Chinese interpreter called them chia-shen, (Tibetan: yū-lā).[45] There are no images of them. Instead, a bunch of hair from various animals hangs in the left rear corner of the tent, which is the home of yū-lā. The hair of all types of domestic animals is used. A tuft of hair is plucked out of each animal for this purpose before it is sold or killed. Thus, the bundle constantly increases in size. After a meal, tea, butter, and milk are smeared on the bundle of hair for the house god.

Small brass or bronze statues of the Lamaistic deities stand on the altar which is found in every tent. The god which seems to be most popular here is called dẑam-lā. He corresponds allegedly to ts'ai shen, the god of wealth of the Chinese popular religion; in accordance with Lamaistic custom, water is regularly offered to this god.[46] Another god who is highly venerated is the one that is thought of as dwelling in hell and judging the souls of the dead. He corresponds to the Chinese yen-lo wang (Indian: yama). The "horse god" (Chinese: ma wang-yeh; Tibetan: dam-dzěn) is also worshiped in the Lamaistic temples and offered sacrifices by the sorcerers, especially when there is a threat of war. He has three heads and is represented in union with his çakti (Sanskrit, female principle). The god of wealth and the house gods are worshiped by men and women alike. I did not learn anything about a worship of the heavens among the Fantzu, nor of the sun, moon, and stars.

---

44. Cf. Schröder, op. cit. This account of the mountain spirit of the Tujen in the Hsi-ning region is noteworthy for the manifold combinations which the spirit can make.

45. Cf. Hermanns, op. cit., p. 48.

46. Cf. Waddell, op. cit., p. 370.

Spirits of the Dead. After death the soul of the deceased may turn into an evil spirit. It may descend into hell (Tibetan: nāl-wā), where it is sentenced by the judge of hell. Just as in China, however, there is a belief in Buddhistic transmigration of souls, and no one is aware of its inconsistency with other beliefs. If a person has led a good life, he can be reborn as an incarnation; if he has been bad, he becomes a woman or an animal, such as a horse, ox, or sheep. In this case belief in the transmigration of souls has mingled with the belief in evil spirits into which the souls of people who have met violent deaths have been transformed.

A characteristic case of this had just occurred among the Mewu Fantzu: the chief had had a younger brother with whom he had quarreled seven or eight years before about the rule of a group of Fantzu. He had had the brother treacherously murdered one day when the latter was riding across the steppes. A short time afterwards marmots made a burrow behind his property, one entrance of which was within his enclosure. This was a surprising and unusual thing, considering the shy nature of marmots. The chief immediately feared that his brother might be among these marmots and proclaimed a general law against hunting them. The law was still being observed, although the sale of marmot pelts brings in a considerable sum of money. This probably meant that the Fantzu shared or at least understood the fear of their chief. On the other hand, the vicious murder which the chief had committed was in no way avenged, since, according to primitive ideas of justice, that concerned the family of the victim exclusively. Ancestor worship is different from that of the Chinese. There are no ancestral tablets. In the Mewu Fantzu dialect the ancestors are called xǒü. After the death of a parent, daily sacrifices are performed in front of the tent. Later, this sacrifice is made only on the first, eighth, fifteenth, and twenty-ninth of the month, and then it is gradually abandoned.

SORCERERS AND MAGIC

Exorcism. Just as Taoist and Buddhist priests practice exorcism, the propitiation of offended spirits and the casting out of evil ones, so Tibetan sorcerers and lamas also engage in this practice. The sorcerer, who corresponds to the Taoist priest (tao shih) or exorcist (kan-kuei hsien-cheng) of the Chinese folk religion, is called nǒ-hua by the Tibetans and bömbu (local pronunciation) by the Chinese. He is a priest of the Bon religion. He wears his hair long and has a special kerchief.[47] There is only one kind

---

47. Cf. H. Hoffmann, Quellen zur Geschichte der Tibetischen Bon-Religion

of sorcerer. Not every tent community has one, and, unfortunately, there was none in the community I visited. The sorcerer marries, and his profession, the art of carrying out exorcistic rites and writing magic formulas to ward off spirits, is handed down from father to son, but not to daughter or son-in-law. The altar in the sorcerer's tent contains the customary small statues of the gods, bowls for holy water, the large Chinese brush with which he writes magic formulas, and long rows of copper coins. The sorcerer also has prayer books, although laymen say that many sorcerers cannot read but only leaf through them. On the other hand, I was told that the sorcerers are able to understand the sacred writings of the lamas, but, conversely, fewer educated lamas understand the sacred writings of the sorcerers. In spite of the high esteem in which the lamas are held, I gathered from the Mewu Fantzu that the magic power of the sorcerer is considered greater than that of the lama, although he does not enjoy special social privileges. In cases of illness the nomads as a rule first consult a lama, who determines which spirit has caused the illness. They are sometimes in doubt whether in a certain case exorcism by a sorcerer or a lama would be more successful. Oddly enough, the result is that a lama is first consulted, and they let him decide by throwing dice which exorcism would be more effective. This is a noteworthy indication of the tolerance Lamaism has for popular religion, and it also shows that the lamas on their part do not doubt the sorcerer's magic power. Thus, I was told that in case of serious illness the sorcerer is generally preferred, because the people believe that he has greater magic power and because he is, nevertheless, no more expensive than a lama.

The most common task of the sorcerer is to heal sickness by magic. The cause of the illness is assumed to be an offense against the spirits, possession by an evil spirit, or enchantment by an enemy. However, sickness is not regarded as a punishment for sin. In our discussion of earth spirits, we pointed out that the Mewu Fantzu believe that sudden illness can arise if one scratches the ground and thereby offends the earth spirits. In this case, barley roasted in a kettle is offered. Half of it is roasted until it is black, and the other half is less thoroughly done. Both halves are mixed and then strewn on the ground. At the same time, cypress wood is

---

(Sources on the History of the Tibetan Bon Religion). ("Akademie der Wissenschaften und der Literatur, Abhandlungen der geistes- und sozial-wissenschaftlichen Klasse" [Transactions of the Division of Humanities and Social Sciences]. [Mainz: 1950]), pp. 137, 197.

burned and sacred writings are read aloud. This reading is an essential part of the ritual of exorcism, just as it is among Chinese exorcists. The sorcerer can read the sacred writings in the tent of the sick person, but he also reads them in his own tent, either to learn them by heart or to bring good luck to people who have commissioned him to do the reading. For a three-day treatment of an illness, the sorcerer is given a sheep or 3 or 4 yuan. For reading sacred writings in his tent throughout a forenoon, he gets about 20 fen. The lama receives the same amount for treating sickness with prayer.

As an exorcist the sorcerer's duty is to drive out evil spirits and, if possible, to destroy them. He has the power to catch evil spirits by reading the sacred writings aloud and using a whip made of yak leather. A man stands in front of the sorcerer and holds a yak-leather bag into which the sorcerer charms the evil spirit. A great many people stand behind the bag, threatening the evil spirit with all kinds of weapons—muskets, bows and arrows, swords, and knives—and driving the spirit into the bag. When the spirit is captured, the bag is carried outside, opened up over a fire of yak dung, and symbolically emptied. The men who accompany the procession threaten the escaping spirit with their weapons, and this is supposed to drive the spirit into the fire, where he is burned. Since this burning of the spirit always takes place at a crossroads, the latter is avoided in the evening because one never knows if the burning has been successful. This type of exorcism is practiced only in cases of illness.

In special cases exorcistic rites are carried on simultaneously by a considerable number of sorcerers. Before a war ten or twenty sorcerers gather to curse the enemy and pray for good fortune. In this case the sorcerers invoke a special deity, the horse god. They may also, like the lamas, invoke the mountain spirits to bring luck, but the ability to practice black magic belongs exclusively to the sorcerers. However, they must be paid more for this than for exorcism. A sorcerer can be induced to bring sickness or a cattle epidemic upon an enemy, but for this he must be paid a yak or a horse, whether or not he is successful.

Black Magic. When black magic is practiced with the help of a sorcerer, a dog is killed and its blood used. The name of the person to be bewitched is written on a slip of paper along with the magic formula. The paper is dipped in the dog's blood and buried near the person who is being bewitched.[48] Meanwhile, the sorcerer reads aloud from the sacred books in his tent. It is not possible to turn men into animals by means of magic or

---

48. The hiding of the objects upon which a curse has been placed to

vice versa, a belief I heard many times in China. If a person believes
that his illness has been caused by a curse, he first has a lama prophesy who
has cast the spell. Then the person lies in wait for the enchanter and shoots
him. My interpreter, who has spent many years with the Mewu Fantzu, had
never actually known any such cases but had heard of them. He maintained,
however, that he knew of several cases of revenge on alleged sorcerers
among the sedentary Fantzu, among whom he had lived at the time. Laymen can protect themselves from black magic not only by availing themselves of the powers of sorcerers and lamas but also by practicing magic
themselves. Any layman who fears magic spells can read the sacred writings,
if he is able to read at all, and thus protect himself against misfortune. The
Fantzu also credit evil persons with the ability to bring about misfortune
such as sickness or cattle epidemics by means of magic.

Strangers are, of course, particularly subject to suspicion. My interpreter learned that after I had come to live among the Mewu Fantzu, they
wondered if an abnormally heavy rain lasting for several days might have
been caused by my visit. The people, particularly the men, were by no
means happy about my visit, especially in the beginning. This suspicion
is not only directed against Europeans but also Chinese, Moslems, and even
Tibetans from the lowlands. The nomads particularly dislike being photo-
graphed or having people make sketches or draw maps. The stranger, especially the European, is highly suspect because of his unusual appearance and
strange customs. This viewpoint is only human and by no means characteristic of Tibetans alone. I found it throughout China. It has been my experience over a period of many years that every slightly unusual event which
coincides with the arrival of a stranger is only too easily regarded as having
been caused by the stranger. This was true whether I was traveling in the
extreme northwestern part of China, in the extreme southeast among the Li
on the island of Hainan, or somewhere in central China.[49]

---

bring about ill luck is a phenomenon which also occurs in China. For example, if a woman wishes her neighbor ill, she tries to gain possession of a
few of the latter's hairs. She brings them to an old woman who is skilled in
the practice of black magic and makes a business of it. With the help of
incantations, the old woman can make the hairs cast an evil spell, for example, cause trachoma or boils. In order to be effective, however, the
hairs must be secretly placed under the chamber pot (ma-t'ung) of the victim.

49. Cf. Sir Charles Bell, Tibet, Past and Present (Oxford: The Clarendon
Press, 1934), p. 207; H. Stübel, Die Li-Stämme der Insel Hainan (The Li
Tribes of the Island of Hainan) (Berlin: Klinkhardt und Biermann, 1937),

Charms and Amulets. The customs observed to ward off or eliminate misfortune or invoke good furtune are a hodgepodge of ideas taken from popular religion and Lamaism. Such customs may be magic practices in the widest sense, linking with all kinds of superstition; they can invoke prayers, sacrifices, or oracles. Amulets are favorite charms; they are preferably made by lamas and consecrated by magic formulas spoken over them. Small strips of silk tied around the throat are sometimes worn as amulets. Among the ornaments worn by the Fantzu, as mentioned above, are rosaries and small, square or round boxes containing sacred objects. These are worn on the chest throughout a lifetime, especially in times of unusual danger, such as war. They are often presented to laymen by lamas.

The amulet boxes worn on the chest contain magic writings of an incarnation, bits of clothing or fingernails, hair, or remnants of the offering of an incarnation, even his excrement; they may contain pills made by the incarnation, which he gives away if one kowtows to him. These pills may also be kept in the tent in front of the family altar. It is believed that after a month or more small pills originate from the initial large one, and these can protect the body from all kinds of disease. Small scraps of clothing of an incarnation are known as nam-sā, the pills, mani-je-lā.

I was unable to get any information about special superstitions relating to unerring marksmanship or imperviousness to bullets. However, I learned of a symbolic act of magic to ward off the threat of war or to bring victory. During my stay among the Mewu Fàntzu, they were very much afraid of the Chinese Communist Army. In the large lamasery of Heh-tso, I observed that hundreds of small figures were being made of a mixture of water, barley flour, and butter, and then were painted red. They were about 10 centimeters high and shaped somewhat like a tripod, pointed at the top. When I asked the meaning of these figures, I got no clear answer. Later I was told that these figures were supposed to represent dead Communists. Symbolic corpses such as these are called lŏn-mā. Armed warriors gathered in the temple and, while the lamas read prayers, they made threatening gestures with their weapons in the direction from which the Communists were expected and struck the "corpses" symbolically. This magic performance is staged before every war.

---

pp. 61, 113, 241; "The Yao of the Province of Kuang Tung," Monumenta Serica, III (1938), 377. Since I have always traveled during the summer, i.e., during the rainy season, I was not at all surprised that the Fantzu connected the rainstorm with my arrival. I had the same experience with a Yao tribe in northern Kuangtung; my guide, a Chinese from the area, was heartily reproached for bringing the rain-bringing stranger. The poor man was soundly thrashed by his fellow citizens after he returned to his village.

Amulets serve to protect animals as well as people. If a Fantzu is worried about the health of a horse, he ties a bundle of bright-colored ribbons in its mane. He buys the ribbons from a lama, who makes them efficacious by means of magic formulas. The sacred yaks and sheep are protected in the same way. The ribbons must be of five different colors: red, yellow, green, blue, and white. They are of cotton or silk, depending on the wealth of the owner.

It was my impression that, apart from the belief in the obos, the magic influence of the configuration of the earth's surface and the distribution of water (which the Chinese call feng-shui), does not seem to be as important to the tent nomads as to the Chinese. The feng-shui is judged only by the lamas, for example, when a tent site is being selected. It is considered unlucky to pitch a tent opposite the main gate of a house, which may happen if one is traveling in the region of the sedentary Fantzu. The most important protection for a tent is the prayer pennant. Within the tent, people are careful not to step over the hearth when they pass from one section of the room to the other. I learned nothing about special superstitions connected with eating or traveling.

Prayer. The frequently mentioned reading aloud of sacred writings by sorcerers, lamas, or laymen may be called prayer. Other important forms of prayer are telling one's beads and the use of prayer pennants and prayer wheels, both of which are specifically Lamaistic. Beads can be counted any time one happens to have a hand free. In almost every tent there is also a hand prayer wheel which usually lies on the altar when it is not in use.[50] It is turned morning and evening by both men and women. One seldom finds stationary wheels that are turned by hand. Among the tent Fantzu I did not see any prayer wheels turned by water or wind power, as I did among the sedentary Fantzu. On the other hand, prayer flags were used a great deal.[51] In front of most tents there is a mast from which two lines adorned with prayer pennants are usually suspended. In cases of illness or other misfortune, the people visit a lama in a monastery and ask his advice. The lama may then recommend the use of a prayer pennant, which is printed by the lama and usually distributed free of charge.

Lamas are called upon to influence the weather by means of prayer, especially when there is too much rainfall or a drought. In that case the lama comes to the tent encampment, pitches his own tent, and reads sacred writings. I did not learn anything about special customs to prevent

---

50. Rockhill, op. cit., pp. 738 f.
51. Ibid., p. 739.

thunderstorms. The sedentary Fantzu leave this to the lamas. Earthquakes are considered a punishment for the wickedness of human beings. When there are eclipses of the sun and moon, the people pray, as they so often do, simultaneously with the lips, rosary, and prayer wheel, and burn juniper wood.

Prayer runs through the entire daily life of the Fantzu. It is usually limited to the Lamaistic formula: "Omi mani padme hum." They mumble this while telling their beads and, if possible, while turning the prayer wheel containing the same formula. This prayer is also written on the prayer pennants found beside every tent. The lama reads prayers for special purposes such as healing the sick. At festivals laymen and lamas repeat common prayers.

Sacrifices. Laymen as well as lamas and sorcerers offer sacrifices to ward off evil influences. On the first, eighth, fifteenth, and twenty-ninth of each month, they burn incense in front of the tent. This custom is observed particularly after a death in order to propitiate the spirits of the ancestors. They burn dwarf juniper and remnants of yak dung in the morning and evening. At the same time, they set out a brass cup containing holy water, butter, and tsamba. The sedentary Fantzu have special clay altars for this purpose; the tent Fantzu burn their offerings on the ground. There are also sacrifices made chiefly to the god of wealth, whose statuette stands on the family altar. They place three bowls to the left and four to the right of this statuette. These are filled every morning with fresh water, as are those in front of a Buddha statue. After the noon meal, the bowls are emptied and stacked.

Sacrifices are made to the mountain spirits on all sorts of occasions chiefly to ward off evil. Offerings include khadaks, arrows for the obo, juniper wood, barley flour, tsamba, butter, holy water in brass bowls, as well as sacrificial paper which, as in China, is burned. Pictures are stamped on the sacrificial paper, as for example, a horse surrounded by the symbols of the "eight treasures." [52] Offerings are also made to the mountain spirit before a hunt, especially when the animals to be hunted are hard to capture, like the musk deer or gazelles. This offering is made on top of the tent and consists of juniper wood, butter, and tsamba. There is another sacrificial rite when war threatens, which undoubtedly goes back to pre-Lamaistic times, and at which lamas are never present. The warriors gather at a place agreed upon and split open with a knife the belly of a

---

52. Cf. Waddell, op. cit., p. 393.

yak, sheep, or goat. The animal is then cast alive on a fire of yak dung and burned to death along with tsamba and butter.

The sacred animals which wealthy people dedicate to the spirits can probably also be regarded as offerings. For this purpose they always choose a male animal (yak or sheep), sometimes one that has been castrated. These animals, which are kept in the owner's herd, may not be shorn or slaughtered; they are allowed to die a natural death. Since people are very much concerned about keeping them well and alive for a long time, they often decorate them with the above-mentioned bundles of colored ribbons which are blessed by the lamas.[53]

Divination. Oracles and prophecies are sought preferably from the lamas. People value them differently. We have mentioned above that the nomads ask a lama to prophesy for them with regard to the driving out of spirits, in order to ascertain whether in a given case this may best be done by a lama or a sorcerer. They also let a lama prophesy how to trace a criminal. The lama may say whether and when the crime may be discovered, and in what direction one must travel to capture the criminal.

Cult of the Altar. The cult of the altar belongs primarily to the Lamaistic religion. In every tent the altar is on the right (male) side, next to the place where the fuel is piled. It is a simple, rectangular wooden box .5 meter high, 40 centimeters deep, and 1.5 meters long. In the middle of the altar stands a small brass statue of Buddha, with three large and three small bowls of water to the left, and four large and four smaller ones to the right. These bowls are supposed to correspond to holes in the heart of Buddha.

Food Taboos. The numerous food taboos can be traced to Buddhist influence. The Fantzu abstain altogether from eating the meat of horses, mules, donkeys, dogs, all fowl and fish, as well as eggs. At present, the meat of marmots is also forbidden. They eat the meat of sheep and yaks, but these animals are not killed in the ordinary way; they are strangled, and thus the crime of shedding blood is avoided.

Life after Death. The strange blend of folk religion and Buddhism (or Lamaism) is expressed very clearly in the ideas which the Mewu Fantzu have about life after death. On the one hand, they worship their ancestors and apparently believe that ancestral souls dwell in some form near the tent, since that is where offerings are regularly presented; they also fear the evil spirits into which the souls of those who have met violent death are transformed. On the other hand, the Buddhist belief in transmigration of

---

53. Cf. Hermanns, op. cit., p. 49.

souls, whereby the soul can be reborn as a human being or animal, is commonly accepted. Thus, the chief's odd fear that the soul of his brother might have entered a marmot and his subsequent decree that marmots were not to be shot, were probably based on the confused mixture of a belief in the transmigration of souls and in the danger of the spirits of human beings who have died a violent death.

Burial Rites. Lamaism has probably had a marked influence on the strange burial rites of the Fantzu. In the vicinity of each lamasery, there are two different elevated burial sites, one for lamas and one for laymen. Immediately after death, the naked corpse is tied in a squatting position and covered with a new felt coat. A person buys the coat himself, or it is given to him by his son or a close relative when he gets old. The corpse is tied together, not by the relatives, but by three men from the neighborhood. The relatives are not present when this is done. The bound corpse is laid either behind a curtain at the entrance to the tent or on the altar box. The next morning before daybreak, the three neighbors return, carry the corpse out of the tent, and tie it on a horse or yak. They lead it to the burial place, taking along tea, tsamba, butter, and mo-mo. They make a pile of yak dung about a foot high at the burial place and place on it a small portion of food offerings, which they burn as a sacrifice. The corpse is laid somewhat below the burnt offering. The greater portion of the food is eaten by the three men, or else it is given to beggars. One of the three men gets as a reward the felt coat in which the deceased was wrapped. Only food offerings, consisting of a little barley and oats, are made if the deceased is a male. These are placed beside the corpse. Women are given cheap ornaments in addition. They are sometimes stolen by Chinese, but never by Fantzu. Only the three attendants go to the burial place. Sometimes beggars are present, but they are very rare in the Fantzu area. The corpse and the burnt offerings attract vultures, and it is usually only a few hours before they appear. The attendants remain at the burial place until the vultures have disposed of the corpse, which happens very quickly since many birds gather.[54] If the vultures do not devour the corpse, the attendants cut it up with a knife, severing the limbs at the joints. Any kind of knife is used for this purpose; afterwards it is washed off and used for other things. The various parts of the corpse are thrown in all directions so that they will be devoured by the vultures. The bones, such as the skull, jaws, and upper thigh bones, are left at the burial place. Many bones are swallowed by the vultures.

---

54. The visual power of the vulture is amazing. Whereas one has not seen any at all, or perhaps only one or two, suddenly a whole flock will appear. This is the surest sign that a funeral is taking place.

While this is going on at the burial place, the relatives and lamas (usually only two of the latter) gather in the tent of mourning, where the lamas read prayers. The family of the deceased prepares a large meal for the lamas and its members. The food consists of tsamba, butter, mo-mo, and meat cooked with rice. After the meal, tsamba and butter are given to the relatives. The lamas continue to read prayers from breakfast until noon, even during the meal. Some time after the death has occurred, the family gives butter, barley flour, and money to the lamasery to which the lamas belong. Wealthy people give each lama 14 yuan, a chin of butter, and a tou of barley flour. Poor people give each lama only 10 fen; the very poor give nothing.

The same ceremonies are performed five or six years after the day of mourning. This custom is probably based on the same ideas as the common second burial in South China. No special mourning clothes are worn. The Fantzu do not customarily weep aloud as the Chinese do at certain funeral ceremonies; only at the funeral feast do they occasionally weep softly, "to be polite and show one's sympathy."

A child's funeral does not differ from that of an adult. If someone has died a violent death, no special customs are observed, nor is there any difference in the case of suicide, but this form of death seems to be rare. My interpreter knew of only two cases of suicide by hanging among the Mewu Fantzu.

After a death has occurred, the Fantzu request an incarnation, or "living Buddha," to perform a ceremony to insure the rebirth of the soul in a human being, not an animal ("scatter flowers of rice," tsou hua mi). The incarnation strews grains of barley all around the tent, forming flower-like figures (Tibetan: dẓam-nǎ). A pointed trivet, a symbol of the dead, is made of tsamba. It is also strewn with barley kernels by the incarnation. A member of the family or a neighbor carries the symbol of the dead out of the tent and throws it away not far from the tent. For this ceremony the incarnation is presented with two yaks, two sheep, and the good clothing of the deceased, depending on the wealth of the relatives. Poor people often give only a small remuneration.

LAMASERIES

In the territory of the Mewu Fantzu there are three lamaseries: the Old and the New Mewu lamaseries and Lao-do-ma, all of which are under the jurisdiction of the Labrang lamasery. Most of the lamas at these places are recruited from among the Mewu Fantzu.[55] However, there are also

---

55. Ekvall, op. cit., p. 37, states that about one out of every three Fantzu men becomes a lama.

some Chinese lamas, mostly people impoverished by the Moslem uprisings in the seventeenth and twenty-first years of the Republic (1928 and 1932). There are more Chinese among the lamas in Heh-tso and in Labrang, and still more in Kumbum, the most famous lamasery of eastern Tibet. According to my interpreter, Chinese lamas are superior to Tibetan lamas, probably because they can read Chinese as well as Tibetan.

The lamaseries have their own pasture lands. They keep no sheep, only yaks, which the young lamas tend. There are no regular taxes collected for the lamaseries, but they are provided with necessary food, most of which is donated at the temple festivals. If a family has a relative who is a lama, it provides him regularly with food. Surplus flour and butter are always sent to the lamasery by people who have a son there. Families connected with the lamaseries take turns defraying the expenses for the temple festivals and supplying the necessary food for these occasions. Lamas also often come to the tents to ask for food, especially butter. A typical feature of nomad life is the appearance of a lama riding from tent to tent to collect butter. These lamas sometimes come from lamaseries outside the Mewu Fantzu territory. An incarnation wearing a golden hat and a red silk sash usually rides at the head of the procession, followed by a few lamas in white hats and one or two mounted laymen to keep off the dogs. When such a group stops in front of a tent, the occupants come out, chain the dogs, and kowtow to the incarnation, who blesses them by touching them with a piece of white cloth. This ceremony brings luck. I felt that the people enjoyed giving the lama surplus butter.

To summarize what we have said about the function of lamas in the everyday religious life of the nomads: the lamas exorcise the evil spirits, chiefly the wicked souls of the dead who bring sickness to man and beast. People come to the lamas to receive amulets as a protection against diseases (of humans and animals) and prayer pennants to protect the tent. Lamas are also requested to exorcise unfavorable weather by reading prayers aloud. Only the lamas can judge feng-shui, the magical influence of the various aspects of landscape on the life of man.

The lamas must recite prayers at festivals, some of which are celebrated by individual families in their tents, others in the lamaseries. They also recite prayers to fend off threats of war. They are consulted when a child is named, one or two months after its birth. First and foremost, the lamas are asked to help in sickness to determine, by casting dice, whether it would be more advantageous to have a lama or a sorcerer exorcise the evil spirit. They are paid a small sum of money for carrying out such exorcisms. If one wants to apprehend a criminal, a lama is asked to prophesy whether the crime can be discovered, when, and in what direction one must travel to capture the criminal. A lama is also consulted if it is believed that an illness was caused by magic. The lama prophesies who has cast the spell.

Aside from all these "religious" functions, a lama's aid is also sought in everyday life, when on any occasion a layman's education is not adequate. If a man closes an important business deal, he asks a lama to help him make out the bill. Most important of all, the scholarly lamas calculate the Chinese calendar for the people and post it on the lamasery gate.

THE INCARNATIONS

The incarnations, or "living Buddhas," have a special significance in the religious life of a lamasery. In Chinese they are called huo-fu, although in Kansu they are most frequently referred to as fu-yeh; in Tibetan they are called ă-lĕ-hă. There are two incarnations at the Old Mewu lamasery and at Lao-do-ma and one at the New Mewu lamasery.[56] The incarnations are sent from Labrang to these temples. They need not come originally from the Mewu Fantzu region. My interpreter could not remember that an incarnation had ever been found among the Mewu Fantzu. He maintained that origin is not important in the selection of an incarnation and that they were not chosen predominantly from the families of tribal chiefs or other influential families. In his opinion they were honestly chosen. The common people have the following to say on the subject: shortly before his death, the incarnation tells his confidant (kuan-chia) where he will be reborn. If he does not mention a specific region or says he will be reborn only after a few years, the kuan-chia consults the great incarnation at Labrang, who figures out when and where the incarnation will be reborn. The kuan-chia takes the deceased incarnation's horsewhip and his wooden tsamba bowl edged with silver and goes into the region indicated by the deceased, or by the incarnation in Labrang, to find the child in which the deceased is reborn. He gives the bowl and whip to a number of children who might be the incarnation. If a child accepts the objects, he is the true incarnation. The child is given khadaks and pulu by the kuan-chia, who then negotiates with the parents concerning the price to be paid for the child. It amounts to several hundred yuan plus some horses and yaks. Often, however, the parents forego compensation because they consider it an honor to have an incarnation in their family. The inhabitants of the region form a cortege and accompany the child to the lamasery he is to enter. The local

---

56. Cf. Waddell, op. cit., pp. 229 ff.

lamas come to meet him. An incarnation is never dismissed, even if he proves unsuitable. No one doubts the genuineness of the method of discovering the incarnation.

The great importance of the incarnation for the lamasery as well as for the religious life of the layman is evident if we consider that each lamasery has a corresponding obo on a sacred mountain, and that the mountain spirit dwelling in the obo is thought of as mystically connected with one of the lamasery's incarnations. The latter, in turn, corresponds to a Buddha or bodhisattva.

The high esteem which the incarnation enjoys among the people gives him a special place in judicial matters: a convicted thief must pay a lama two or three times the indemnity a layman can command, but he must pay an incarnation nine times as much. At New Year's, not only are offerings made to the mountain spirit at the obo but also a festival attended by laymen is held at the lamaseries, at which fireworks are set off in honor of the former incarnation. The Tibetan regards it as a special reward for a sinless life to be reborn as an incarnation, although he does not realize that this view contradicts the essential nature of an incarnation. As we said above, people like to give butter to the incarnation when he comes to the encampment to request food for the lamasery.

FESTIVALS

There are four annual religious festivals in the lamaseries: from the first to the fifteenth of the first month; from the fifteenth to the twenty-fifth of the fifth month; from the first to the fifteenth of the eighth month; and from the fifteenth to the twenty-fifth of the tenth month, according to the Chinese calendar. There are no other religious festivals, with the exception of the festival known as "speaking and sitting silent." No religious festivals are celebrated in the tents. However, during the lamasery festivals, or shortly thereafter, people invite friends and relatives to their tents. The laymen bring meat, wine, and money to the festivals as gifts for the lamasery; no gifts are brought when people are invited into the tents. The wine is drunk only by the laymen, never by lamas. At the New Year's festival, which as a rule lasts a fortnight, feasts are usually prepared in the tents, but only on the first three days. This festival was formerly simpler among the Fantzu, but it has been influenced by the Chinese. On the morning of New Year's Day, they burn cypress wood as a sacrifice to the mountain spirits. On the fourth day of the year, everybody goes to the lamasery where a large feast consisting mostly of mo-mo, soft, flat rolls about 30

48

centimeters in diameter, and butter is given. Fireworks are set off in honor of the deceased incarnations. At the same time, a festival is held on the obo mountain to invoke the ami. Butter, tea, mutton, and cypress wood are offered. At the New Year's feasts in the tents, beef, mutton, and pork are eaten, as well as butter, a kind of bread made of unroasted barley flour, pastry baked in oil, and tsamba. In addition, they buy bean flour, noodles, carrots, and cabbage in Ho-chou. If the family is wealthy, they also eat pao-tzu (dumplings filled with garlic), a dish similar to ravioli. It is popular all over North China. Noodles and mo-mo are also served exclusively at New Year's and on other festive occasions. The family drinks wine if it can afford it.

Besides the festivals described above, the niu-nä festival is held annually in summer, but only among the nomads of the Mewu tribe. The name of the festival means "speaking and sitting silent." The site of the festival, a shallow valley in the grasslands with steep, pointed limestone peaks in the background, is always the same. The time of the festival is determined each year by the New Mewu lamasery. In order that the live-stock may prosper throughout the year, a festival is held to honor the spirits; prayers are offered for favorable wind and sufficient rain. There is no special offering during the five-day festival. At least one or two persons, usually more, from each family, men and women, old people and youngsters, participate. Each family is required to send at least one representative. If it fails to do so, it must pay a fine. Only about twenty or thirty people arrive on the first day to erect the tents for the participants. The tents stand at the edge of the festival grounds and measure about one hundred meters in diameter. There is also a beautiful, rectangular temple tent in which the lamas say their prayers. It is decorated with a three-colored cloth frieze and black ornaments. Inside there are pictures of saints and an altar. Next to the temple there are two larger tents which serve as the common kitchen. Most of the participants' tents are made of the customary coarse, black tent cloth. Only the wealthy people pitch small white tents of the type the lamas use on their travels.

Most of the participants arrive on the second day. They do not eat anything in the morning but do take liquids. Towards noon as large a meal as possible is served, including tsamba, butter, rice, and sour milk, but no wine. Mo-mo baked in oil and butter is the main dish. The meal lasts one or two hours because enough must be eaten for two days. The mo-mo are baked on a large common hearth; the ingredients, wheat flour and rape oil purchased in Labrang or Ho-chou, are collected from the tents. The mo-mo are distributed equally among all the participants. When they eat, men and women sit on the ground in two rows facing one another. The occupants of

49

one tent, seven to ten persons, sit together. After the meal, they fast and are silent for the rest of the day. On the third day of the festival, they neither eat nor talk; only prayers are mumbled by men and women. On the fourth day, there is again a large meal, but otherwise no one eats or converses. On the fifth day, the conduct is the same as on the third: fasting, prayer, silence. On the sixth day, the festival breaks up. I visited it on the fourth day, and my impression was that the participants were in a very quiet, dull, and somewhat sleepy mood.

The festival is conducted by the lamas of the Mewu lamaseries, more than half of whom attend. The chief usually does not come himself, but always sends members of his family. The participants arrive in their best clothes, often in magnificent peasant costumes. The women wear red silk tassels on their conical felt hats. You see a great many purple and scarlet silk jackets with gay collars; red, purple, and figured pulu coats; and costly hair ornaments of silver and gold. The central section of the girls' gala hair ornaments is decorated with bands of silver leaf. The women's coats are often trimmed with a striped flounce resembling a skirt and edged with otter fur or colored cloth. Everyone brings along his best saddles and bridles, which are mounted with silver. You see many showy weapons, guns with silver-mounted stocks, and swords in choice sheaths. The women also wear beautiful knives in their belts.

FAMILY LIFE

Names. Mewu Fantzu are said to have surnames (hsing). This custom was probably taken over from the Chinese only a very short time ago since the use of the surname is not customary among the Fantzu. It is also not used in conversation.[57] According to an ancient custom, a child is given a name by a lama when it is one or two months old. This name-giving is not connected with a special festival. An adult is usually given a nickname by his friends, which refers to a special characteristic or event, for example, "imperfection" or "deformed." I received no information about a change of name at the time of marriage.

Marriage. People with the same surname may marry, as may relatives with the exception of brothers and sisters. Thus, cousins may marry, or a nephew may marry his aunt on either side of the family, or a son may

---

57. Ekvall, op. cit., p. 42, and Rockhill, op. cit., p. 724, state that the Amdo-Tibetans have only given names.

50

marry the divorced wife of his father. One may marry someone from the immediate neighborhood or an outlying district; one is not bound to marry members of a certain encampment or family.

The marriage age, as a rule, is between the fifteenth and the eighteenth year. There is considerable sexual intercourse before marriage, and a couple marries when a child is born. There are love matches and matches arranged by a go-between. Even in the case of marriage for love, the go-between is sent by the young man to the family of his beloved.

If there is only one son, he becomes a lama. If there are two sons, the older one stays at home, and the younger becomes a lama; often all the sons except the first-born enter a lamasery. Sometimes all the sons join a lamasery. In that case, or if there is no son, a son-in-law must be adopted. These sons-in-law are, as a rule, ex-lamas who did not like the life of the lamasery. Thus, there is always a shortage of eligible males. On the other hand, there are no older unmarried women. Polygyny is uncommon except among very wealthy people. Polyandry, which occurs in parts of Tibet, is not customary among the Mewu Fantzu. The sons who become lamas are sent into the lamasery when they are eight or ten years old.

Among the Mewu Fantzu, the nomads and the sedentary Fantzu intermarry. It is said that a nomad gains in prestige by marrying a woman from a sedentary family[58] The latter is pleased with such a match provided her husband is wealthy. Conversely, a sedentary Fantzu can marry a nomad woman without being discredited. The nomads also intermarry with Chinese and Moslems. The Mongols living in the province of Kansu have no contact with the Mewu Fantzu.

A Chinese or a Moslem may marry a nomad woman, but a nomad will not marry a Chinese woman because she does not understand the work a nomad woman has to perform. A family of nomads gains in social standing if a Chinese marries into the family. Hence, the nomads do not always demand a dowry from the Chinese or at any rate not a large one. Usually, the Chinese is obliged to give only a yak.

If it is a love match, neither the parents nor other relatives have any influence in the choice of the husband. The wedding gift is paid in yaks and consists of one to five yaks, depending on the wealth of the man's family. If a son-in-law is adopted, the girl's family must give her betrothed's family one or two yaks, provided the son does not come from a family living far away. In this case nothing need be paid.

---

58. Ekvall, op. cit., pp. 76-77, says exactly the opposite, that the nomads are always held in higher esteem than the sedentary Fantzu.

The wedding celebration varies, depending upon whether a woman marries into the man's family or whether a son-in-law is adopted. In the former instance, the bride rides to her husband's tent on the wedding day wearing a new, dark- or light-blue cotton coat (very occasionally, a red one) over her sheepskin coat. She is accompanied by the go-between, her sisters, and young men and women from the neighborhood. When they arrive at the tent, there are no particular ceremonies as there are at Chinese weddings, where fireworks are set off and musicians blow their horns. The bride is received in front of the tent by a neighbor of the bridegroom. The latter does not come out of the tent. These people have not adopted any Chinese marriage ceremonies, such as kowtowing to the parents-in-law, to the ancestors, and to heaven and earth. The woman, with her attendants, enters the left side of the tent, and a sumptuous wedding feast begins that lasts from morning to evening. It is shared by the relatives of the bride and groom. The relatives of the bride bring wine and money for the wedding feast. Naturally, the men sit on the right and the women on the left side of the tent during the feast. They occasionally sing, but there is neither musical accompaniment nor dancing. The food consists chiefly of mo-mo baked in butter, meat, and tsamba, with wine to drink. I did not learn of any other wedding customs. Unfortunately, I had no opportunity to be present at a wedding.

When the bridegroom is adopted into the family of the bride, his future father-in-law fetches him from the tent of his family. The bridegroom's relatives accompany him to the tent of his adopted parents, or parents-in-law. His father-in-law presents him with a rifle, a horse, and a pulu coat. The feast is the same as the one described above, except that the relatives of the bride give no money or presents at the wedding feast.

Childbirth. Directly after the birth of a child, the woman goes to the nearest brook to fetch a tub of water, which she carries home on her back, believing that a heavy burden is beneficial to her health. She often does not have any kind of help during childbirth. The baby is not washed after birth. The mother may not eat sour milk or anything cold; she must drink sweet, warm milk and, if possible, eat only good cooked mutton. If the father has time, he helps his wife prepare meals during the first few days; otherwise he need not observe any particular customs. The woman does not receive special callers. The Fantzu rejoice equally over the birth of a boy or a girl, since a girl can later bring an adopted son into the household. There are no festivals after a child is born; nor are there any initiation ceremonies when a youth reaches maturity.

Position of Women. The woman always has a decisive voice within the family, whether her husband was adopted by her family or whether she married into her husband's family. In commercial transactions the woman has the final decision; if possible the man asks her approval before concluding any business deal. Sometimes the woman beats her husband, but beatings are often reciprocal. Relatives cannot interfere in a marriage. If young couples cannot get along, the chief makes the decision at the divorce proceedings.

After the death of his wife, a man can remarry immediately provided he has the necessary means; a widow can also remarry at once. Orphans are taken in by the grandparents, if possible, or by the nearest relatives. If his wife dies, a man keeps his children provided that the wife has married into his family. If a man who has been adopted into the wife's family dies, the children remain with her family, even if this family should adopt a second husband for her. If the widow of an adopted husband marries into another family, the children of the first marriage remain with her family. If an adopted son-in-law dies, the family tries to find a new husband for the widow as soon as possible. The new son-in-law then inherits the property of the first husband, but he must also provide for the children of the first marriage. If the family cannot soon adopt a husband for a widow, or if she marries into another family, her grown son becomes the heir. She herself has no right to the personal fortune of her deceased husband, even if she has no grown son. In that case, her husband's property is distributed equally among his relatives and neighbors under the chief's supervision. Otherwise, the incarnation of the district lamasery inherits the property, which he resells if he cannot use it himself. The personal property of a deceased mother is divided equally among her daughters and daughters-in-law. If there are no female survivors, it is sold and the proceeds go to the nearest relatives.

POLITICAL ADMINISTRATION

The territory of the Mewu Fantzu was formerly part of the Tibetan province of Amdo, which became the province of Tsinghai and part of Kansu. The word "Amdo" is still applied to the region west of the pasture lands of the Mewu Fantzu. Formerly, the seat of the government was in the old part of Taochow. After the district of Hsia-ho was established ten years ago, the territory came under its administration. The district city of Hsia-ho developed from the market town that sprang up next to the Labrang lamasery. The Fantzu who belong to the Labrang lamasery are called Nan-fan erh-shih-szu tsu, and the Mewu Fantzu are a tribe belonging to this group. It is said that a total of 108 lamaseries are subordinate to the great incarnation at Labrang. Only 3 of these are in the territory of the Mewu Fantzu.

At the head of the Mewu Fantzu is a tribal chief known as t'ou-mu (sometimes as t'u-szu). He has the title of Mewu huan-pu. There are said to be 150 tent encampments under his jurisdiction, plus the sedentary Mewu Fantzu. An encampment consists of ten to forty tents. These figures seem very high to me, considering the extremely sparse settlement of the Mewu Fantzu territory.

The chief of the Mewu tribe is responsible to the Chinese district magistrate (hsien-chang) of Hsia-ho in administrative matters; to Commander Huang, the present feudal lord of Labrang, in military matters; and to the Labrang lamasery in religious matters. The feudal lord is in control of a large area of which the Mewu Fantzu territory is a part. Even after the fall of the Manchu Dynasty, the feudal lord maintained considerable independence in the Chinese-governed border areas inhabited by non-Chinese people (Tibetans, Lolo, Tai). Taxes were paid to him, and in case of war he could recruit soldiers from their region. Originally, the Chinese government played the role of supreme liege lord, since the feudal lords had to pay taxes to it and lend assistance in war. The Chinese government installed the feudal lord in office; that is to say, it gave to a particular family its domain as an hereditary feudal possession to a certain extent. Commander Huang was installed only seven or eight years ago (about 1928) by the Chinese government. His family, known for its warlike (or rather marauding) enterprises, comes from the province of Sikang. It is characteristic of the intellectual and social attitude of a feudal society that the highest incarnation of the Labrang lamasery is a brother of Commander Huang. The independence of the Commander was very much curtailed by the Chinese government, especially after the organization of the district of Hsia-ho. The Mewu chief and subchiefs henceforth did not have to pay taxes to the feudal lord but transferred them directly to the Chinese district officials.

One of the lamaseries in the territory of the Mewu Fantzu, the New Mewu lamasery, is directly under the administration of the chief. The territory of the Old Mewu lamasery is under the administration of three subchiefs. The territory of Lao-do-ma is under two subchiefs, one of whom has a higher rank than the other. Sedentary as well as nomad Fantzu are under the administration of these subchiefs.

The chief lives alternately in a house situated between Heh-tso and the New Mewu lamasery or in a tent which is no different from the tents of other Fantzu. He has a representative in each of the three lamaseries in his area and sometimes lives with them. The office of the chief is hereditary from father to eldest son; but if this son is not suited to the position, the father has the right to name a better qualified son as his successor. If the chief has no sons, his adopted son-in-law becomes his successor. A definite number of families are under the administration of the chief and each of his five subchiefs. Each of these families has a right to five pasture areas. There are no marriage restrictions within the group of families governed by the chief. The chief must see to it that no people from a strange tribe pasture their animals in the region under his jurisdiction. He has more than ten officials (Chinese: kuan-shih) who are laymen and, in addition, the above-mentioned representatives in the lamaseries. They too are known as kuan-shih, although they are lamas. Their task, among other things, is to welcome lamasery guests. There are no particular office-holders apart from the chief, his five subchiefs, and the kuan-shih. Since the chief does not speak Chinese, he has a Chinese secretary to deal with the district officials. He communicates with the secretary through an interpreter. The chief appoints the kuan-shih and discharges them if they are not qualified. A kuan-shih is not paid, but one is obliged to accept the post if appointed by the chief. Length of office is not determined; it runs between one and two years. The kuan-shih must help the chief carry out his duties. For example, they are sent by him to some tent community to conduct inquiries in legal matters, such as the investigation of a robbery. The tent communities do not have any local government.

The main duties of the chief are as follows: he regulates the distribution of pasture land and determines when the nomads are to move from one pasture to another. The oat fields in the region of the winter pasture lands are his property and apportioned by him. Rent, usually in the form of butter, must be paid to him for the oat fields. He is the war lord of the tribe and as such can recruit eligible men for military service as well as mounts and pack animals (horses and yaks). In case of war, he must put his soldiers at the disposal of the feudal lord of Labrang. He and his subchiefs must collect the taxes levied by the Chinese government and hand them over to the district official of Hsia-ho. I could not ascertain whether the chief withholds a certain amount of the taxes for himself. He must also put mounts and pack animals at the disposal of the Chinese district official when the latter or one of his subordinates travels through the territory of the Mewu Fantzu. The chief has the same prerogatives as an incarnation in that he can demand a nine-fold indemnity if he has been robbed. He also has the privilege of donating the largest branch of a bush and a particularly long arrow at the obo festival.

From what we have said about the position and authority of the tribal chief, it follows that he and his officials have no particular influence on the members of a tribe. We have also mentioned that the individual tent communities do not have regular chiefs. As far as I could ascertain, the clan has no great influence in the social and judicial life. There are no clan chiefs like the Chinese tsu chang.

On the other hand, certain societies have been formed which are given the general name of t'saowa[59] and whose chief function seems to be to provide legal protection. The t'saowa of the Mewu nomads consists of four groups. There are 40 to 100 families or tents in each group, which chooses its own leader. There are no rules about the length of time the leader of a group remains in office, nor can the chief influence the choice of such a leader. The individual groups are named after their leaders. The power of each group within the tribe varies. Often a certain family strives to shift from a less influential group to a more influential one; they can do this by presenting the group leader and several respected members of the group with a sheep and several chin of wine and inviting them to a meal. The leader, together with the entire group, is responsible for each crime committed by one of its members. He carries on negotiations with the leader of another group if one of its members is obliged to pay a fine to a member of his group for some crime. The leader of the group whose member has committed the offense must exact the fine from the criminal and give it to the leader of the victim's group. If a member of one group cannot pay a penalty demanded of him, the entire group guarantees to raise the fine. The guilty person must then gradually pay off the debt to the members of his group. The t'saowa can oust a criminal whom they consider onerous; the only thing he can then do is to join another group. I could not find out to what extent this is possible. Apparently there are never disagreements between the chief and a group or its leader about verdicts and penalties.

SOCIAL CHARACTERISTICS

During my brief sojourn with the Mewu Fantzu, I was naturally unable to form a definite, objective opinion of their character, partially due to my ignorance of their language and even more to their unfriendly attitude towards strangers. Despite the fact that they knew my interpreter and did not dislike him, I had to spend considerable time on general topics before I could ask more detailed questions about their way of life. I should like to

---

59. Ekvall, op. cit., p. 69, mentions these groups briefly and calls them "thsu-ba." I have given the pronunciation of my Chinese interpreter.

insert here a few statements of my interpreter, who judged the Fantzu from the point of view of a simple, but intelligent Chinese trader. Naturally he unwittingly made comparisons with the Chinese conditions of life under which he grew up, but I did feel that he made an effort to be neutral in his judgment. In any case, he had had no particularly bad experiences during all the years of his contact with the Fantzu and was not prejudiced against them, as is often the case with Chinese, who cannot suppress a certain arrogance towards people of other cultures.

My interpreter described the Mewu Fantzu as generally honest, courteous, and hospitable. They do not anger very easily; they are faithful in friendship and very willing to help each other. Being a Chinese, my interpreter was very scornful of their lack of piety toward their parents. Sometimes an adult son refuses to take his parents into his tent. For this reason, one occasionally sees old people begging at temples or burial places. Even wealthy people sometimes treat their parents badly. The Fantzu do not often lie nor do they incline to boasting; on the contrary, they try to belittle their property and put little value on "face." Even wealthy people wear dirty clothes and sometimes even beg. They do not forget insults. In business the Fantzu are less reliable than the Chinese. They often do not keep their promises and sometimes forget to pay.

CRIME

The most common crimes are: theft, armed robbery, the infliction of body injuries, and, in the opinion of the Fantzu themselves, black magic. Fantzu law is unwritten and based on custom. The tribal chief, to whom all serious legal cases are presented, makes decisions, usually with the approval of the t'saowa groups. According to my interpreter, the Fantzu do not have a tendency to steal, or at any rate they do not rob each other. If they accept a stranger into their midst, they do not steal from him or rob him, especially if he is a guest.[60] Inconsistent though it seemed, my interpreter was always very careful about guarding my belongings, which were stored in the tent so that they could not be easily reached from the outside. An American missionary assured me that this precaution was justified for he had lived a great deal among the Fantzu and had often been robbed.

---

60. This was my case as I had come with introductions from the Labrang monastery.

Nevertheless, my interpreter's insistence that the Fantzu do not tend to steal is only an apparent contradiction. Wherever primitive ideas of justice prevail, stealing from strangers is judged on a different moral basis than theft from members of one's own group. Even very primitive peoples like the pygmies of the Congo jungle are extremely honest among themselves, whereas as soon as they come into contact with Negro farmers they quickly develop into clever thieves.[61] The line of distinction between the extortionist tourist industry, which is not regarded as criminal, and the robbing of strangers by natives cannot be clearly drawn.

If a thief is caught and confesses at once, he is merely forced to return or replace the stolen goods provided the victim does not belong to the same t'saowa group. If he will not confess, he may be brought to the chief's court and tortured until he confesses. Even then the punishment is no more severe. If the owner of the stolen goods belongs to the same group, the thief must pay him back two or three times their value, the same amount he would have to pay to a lama. A chief or incarnation must be repaid ninefold. [62]

Outside their tribal territory, all Fantzu tend to rob, especially travelers. However, robberies no longer occur as much among the Mewu Fantzu as among tribes living farther in the interior of Tibet, where robberies are the order of the day. According to my interpreter, the Fantzu do not generally shoot or become violent during an assault if no resistance is offered. In that respect they do not act any differently from Chinese robbers.[63]

Quarrels leading to manslaughter occur more often among the Mewu Fantzu than among the neighboring Chinese, according to my interpreter. The Fantzu tend to violence when they are drunk. Murder also occurs, the motives being jealousy or covetousness. It also happens that a man shoots another because he honestly believes he has been the victim of black magic.

---

61. M. Gusinde, Die Kongo-Pygmäen in Geschichte und Gegenwart (The Congo Pygmies Throughout History and the Present) ("Nova Acta Leopoldina, N. F.," Vol. 2 [Halle: 1942]).

62. Cf. A. Musil, The Manners and Customs of the Rwala Bedouins ("American Geographical Society. Oriental Explorations and Studies No. 6" [New York: 1928]).

63. A Szechwan farmer described this behavior of robbers as k'e-ch'i, or "polite," whereas it would be impolite, in his opinion, to shoot directly at people who could not defend themselves, or to behave violently in any way.

If a murder has been committed, the family of the victim does not relax its efforts until it has avenged itself on the murderer, if possible by killing him. Blood revenge may be taken if manslaughter has been committed in a state of intoxication, or if a person suspected of black magic has been killed. If blood revenge is not taken, the family suffers loss of respect. However, it rarely occurs in actual fact, for the murderer usually flees beyond the borders of the tribal territory and seeks refuge with another tribe. If the murderer is caught before the victim's family can avenge itself, he is soundly thrashed and held captive until he can pay a penalty of eighty yaks. Thereupon, he is banished from tribal territory for four years. The death penalty is not inflicted except by a murdered man's kin. The property of the murderer is seized whether he is captured or escapes. Blood revenge is not considered murder, nor is it punished. The custom of blood revenge among the Mewu Fantzu is hardly alive today. It seems to have been replaced by an indemnity in the form of yaks. For example, if a member of a t'saowa group kills a member of another, the leaders of the two groups decide on the indemnity, usually a penalty of eighty yaks, at least forty of which must be first class. The rest may be somewhat inferior. If the relatives of the criminal cannot meet the full payment, the entire group must make up the deficit.

PROPERTY RIGHTS

In matters of property rights, the nomads naturally place the question of the right to pasture land in the foreground. Pasture lands are divided among the tent communities by the tribal chief. Land for cultivating oats is divided among the individual families. Everyone may cultivate all he needs for his stock. The chief divides the various families into tent communities. The boundaries of the various tent communities must be respected just as strictly as those of the entire tribe. There are also fixed rules about the use of pastures during the different seasons. The tent communities do not quarrel over pasture lands. Violations of pasture land rules are punished with a fine which must be paid in butter. For every yak that breaks out of its pasture, its owner must pay two chin of butter. The lamaseries have their own pastures for yaks; they do not raise sheep.

There seem to be no particular hunting rights, but the chief has the authority to forbid hunting under certain circumstances. During my stay among the Mewu Fantzu the shooting of marmots was forbidden for definite reasons (see section on spirits of the dead). In such cases, permission to hunt is not granted, even for money. If a person is caught violating the law, he is first beaten and then required to pay a fine.

Written contracts are not used in business transactions. Stock is sold by the head. The Fantzu are very astute businessmen; in general they do not quarrel over business transactions.

JUDICIAL AUTHORITY OF THE CHINESE ADMINISTRATION

Judicial authority is only theoretically in the hands of the Chinese administration; in practice it is left to the Fantzu. The Chinese court does not prosecute punishable actions of the Fantzu. Even when a Fantzu has wronged a Chinese, he is not prosecuted directly by a Chinese court but by the chief at the request of the district official. The chief is the highest magistrate. Only when very influential Chinese have been robbed, do the Chinese authorities send out a military posse. The Chinese do not dare harm the Fantzu since they are afraid of revenge. They are glad when the Fantzu leave them alone. Two years ago, Chinese soldiers killed seven or eight Fantzu, whereupon the chief immediately sent out his warriors to pursue them. However, there was no fighting because a Moslem officer acted as mediator. A fine of 100 yuan was paid for each man slain. The incident shows that the Moslem played a neutral and respected role as mediator between the Fantzu and the Chinese. The chief can prosecute a crime only if it takes place within his tribal borders. If the criminal escapes into another territory, he may not pursue him further.

The leaders of the t'saowa groups have about the same social standing as the chief. Their task is a little more arduous since in judicial cases and in the pursuit of a criminal, they are appealed to first. The leader, however, is required to ask the chief for permission to pursue a criminal. As a rule the chief and the groups work together in such cases.

LEGAL PROCEDURE

In legal disputes, the chief chooses a body of judges consisting of himself, the group leaders, and the kuan-shih, or other mature men known to be good speakers and fair in their judgment. The number of judges varies according to the importance of the case. The choice of venue depends on the circumstances; usually the trial is held in a temple or a sedentary Fantzu village. Witnesses are examined much as in a Chinese court. The parties must swear before a Buddha image to tell the truth. If the truth cannot be ascertained from witnesses, various methods of trial by ordeal are used. In less serious cases, a box containing a black and a white stone is produced.

The person who draws the white stone wins. In more serious cases, one of two forms of trial by ordeal is used: the two parties must either touch a red-hot ax with their hands, or they must dip their hands into boiling rape oil. The one whose hand is not burned is innocent. The latter test is the one most often used.

If the accused will not confess, he is tortured. There are nine different methods of torture: 1. A person is whipped on the back with a leather whip. 2. His hands are tied behind his back with a leather strap, and he is suspended from a post by his hands. 3. Both wrists are bound with a rope made of yak hair, whereupon eight men, four on either side, pull the rope tight. 4. His arms and legs are stretched out, and he is suspended in the air; in this position he is lashed on the back with a whip. 5. His back and legs are beaten with willow withes. 6. He is whipped with a leather whip. If after the sixth punishment the accused does not confess, he is acquitted and receives a horse as indemnity. The third form of torture is the most dreaded. Three additional forms of punishment occur under certain circumstances: 7. The legs of the accused are tied together, and he is dragged along the ground. The eighth and ninth methods of torture consist of lashings. The chief orders the torture to take place after he has consulted the court. He can appoint anyone he chooses to inflict the torture.

As we have said, there is no capital punishment except blood revenge. Imprisonment is unknown, although the chief may incarcerate a criminal until trial has taken place. Infractions of any kind are atoned for by the payment of fines in money, butter, sheep, or yaks. If a convicted person cannot pay the imposed penalty, the chief has him arrested and soundly thrashed. The unpaid penalty must be made good by the group. The accused must gradually pay back the group. The most severe punishment is probably expulsion from the group, which makes a man homeless.

Witnesses are not tortured. They are not examined in public but in a separate room so that they cannot be seen by the accused and thus be exposed to his revenge.

The chief also has jurisdiction over members of another tribe and may punish them. However, the punishment is not always recognized by the tribe of the convicted person. During my stay among the Mewu Fantzu, the chief had held a lama prisoner for stealing a rifle and had ordered him whipped. The lama belonged to the Heh-tso monastery, outside Mewu territory. Because of the chief's actions, no male Mewu Fantzu ventured into the region of Heh-tso since he would have risked being captured.

Disputes between members of various families in a community are settled by the chief or one of the kuan-shih, as are disputes between different communities. Violence is seldom resorted to in such cases. Disputes between sedentary and nomadic Fantzu are very rare. These too are settled by the chief. On the other hand, there are quarrels between Fantzu of different tribes, which sometimes lead to war.

WAR

In former times, wars were frequent. The Mewu Fantzu fought their last war about thirty years ago in Imperial times. A war was fought just a few years ago about a hundred li to the southwest. It lasted three years and ended only when the ruling feudal lord of Labrang seized power. If a state of war arises, such as the one during my visit when the district between Taochow and Ho-chou (which includes the territory of the Mewu Fantzu and the lamaseries of Labrang and Heh-tso) was endangered by the Communists, the military commander calls out his chiefs. They recruit soldiers. Every tent must furnish at least one soldier, sometimes as many as two or three. Each man must bring his own weapons, ammunition, and horses, just as in ancient times in the wars of nomadic peoples such as the Khitan and the Mongols. Families who cannot furnish a soldier must give rifles and other weapons, ammunition, and a horse for those who are too poor to furnish their own equipment. The chiefs decide how dangerous the situation is and how many recruits are to be mustered.

RELATIONS WITH THE CHINESE AND THE MOSLEMS

To summarize, it may be said with regard to the political relationship between the Mewu Fantzu and the Chinese, that the Mewu Fantzu are, to a certain extent, dependent on the Chinese since they live relatively near them. This dependence is, however, still a rather indirect one. The secular ruler of Labrang, Commander Huang, is the link between the Mewu Fantzu and the Chinese.

Wars between the Fantzu and the Chinese no longer occur since the Fantzu respect the superior military might of the Chinese. It often happens, however, that Chinese are robbed by Fantzu. Such cases as a rule are brought before the court of Commander Huang, who, according to my Chinese interpreter, sides with the Fantzu whenever possible. He arranges the payment of damages. The Fantzu are not on the whole too friendly with the Chinese: first of all, because they feel oppressed by the taxes the Chinese government imposes upon them; secondly, because the Chinese are pushing into their territory as colonists. However, this second reason is of practical importance only to the sedentary Fantzu.

The Fantzu have a different and closer relationship with the Chinese Moslems, who play a special part in the political and social life of the country.[64] In language and material culture these Moslems do not differ from actual Chinese, but the latter regard them more or less as aliens. They are largely descendants of Turkish tribes who in the course of time settled in Kansu and intermarried with the Chinese. They are of the Turanian race rather than Sinic.[65] They are often very different from the Chinese in external appearance as well as in character. The Moslems live in Kansu as farmers, merchants, and innkeepers. As traders they have penetrated far into the Fantzu territory and constitute the chief population element in the market towns which have arisen near the lamaseries. If Moslems are robbed by Fantzu, they are much more likely to follow their natural warlike bent and fight than are the Chinese. Thus, Fantzu raids are sometimes followed by minor avenging expeditions on the part of the Moslems. Eleven years ago the last major warlike entanglement occurred between the Moslems and the Fantzu. The relationship of the Moslems to the Chinese is more tense. Until very recently there were often bloody Moslem uprisings against the Chinese government. The last of these took place about eight years before my trip in 1928. In such times of unrest, when the power of the Chinese officials is not very strong, there is a general feeling of great insecurity. The Fantzu often take the opportunity to plunder the Chinese, although the Chinese who fled into the Fantzu territory during the last uprising were well treated by the Fantzu. Since then the amiable relationship between the Chinese and the Fantzu has deteriorated more and more so that in 1936 my interpreter doubted whether the Fantzu would assist the Chinese in a Moslem uprising.

---

64. Ekvall, op. cit., describes in detail the relationships among the Fantzu, Chinese, and Moslems.

65. These terms stem from E. von Eichstedt, Rassenkunde und Rassengeschichte der Menscheit (The Study of Races and the Racial History of Mankind) (Stuttgart: 1937-54).

BIBLIOGRAPHY

Bell, Charles Alfred. Tibet, Past and Present. Oxford: Clarendon Press, 1934.

Eickstedt, E. von. Rassenkunde und Rassengeschichte der Menscheit (The Study of Races and the Racial History of Mankind). Stuttgart, 1937-54.

Ekvall, Robert B. Cultural Relations on the Kansu-Tibetan Border. The University of Chicago Publications in Anthropology, Occasional Papers, No. 1. Chicago: University of Chicago Press, 1939.

Futterer, K. Durch Asien (Through Asia). Geographische Charakter-Bilder (Geographical Sketches), Vol. I. Berlin: Dietrich Reimer, 1901.

Gusinde, Martin. Die Kongo-Pygmäen in Geschichte und Gegenwart (The Congo Pygmies Throughout History and the Present). Nova Acta Leopoldina, N.F., Vol. II. Halle, 1942.

Hermanns, Matthias. Die Nomaden von Tibet (The Nomads of Tibet). Vienna, 1949.

Hoffmann, H. Quellen zur Geschichte der Tibetischen Bon-Religion (Sources on the History of the Tibetan Bon Religion). Akademie der Wissenschaften und der Literatur, Abhandlungen der geistes- und sozialwissenschaftlichen Klasse (Transactions of the Division of Humanities and Social Sciences). Mainz, 1950.

Li An-che. "A Lamasery in Outline," Journal of the West China Border Research Society, XIV, Series A, 35-68. Chengtu: Yung Hsing Cooperative Press, 1942.

Musil, Alois. The Manners and Customs of the Rwala Bedouins. American Geographical Society, Oriental Explorations and Studies, No. 6. New York, 1928.

Rockhill, William Woodville. Notes on the Ethnology of Tibet. Report of the U. S. National Museum for 1893, pp. 665-747. Washington: Government Printing Office, 1895.

Schröder, Dominik. "Zur Religion der Tujen des Sininggebietes (Kukunor)" (Contributions to the Religion of the Tujen of the Hsi-ning Region, Ch'inghai), Anthropos, Vol. XLVII. Freiburg, 1952.

Stübel, H. Die Li-Stämme der Insel Hainan (The Li Tribes of the Island of Hainan). Berlin: Klinkhardt und Biermann, 1937.

----. "The Yao of the Province of Kuang Tung," Monumenta Serica, Vol. III. Peiping: Henri Vetch, 1938.

Tafel, Dr. Albert. Meine Tibetreise (My Tibetan Trip). 2 vols. Stuttgart: Union Deutsche Verlagsgesellschaft, 1914.

Waddell, L. Austine. The Buddhism of Tibet or Lamaism. London: W. H. Allen, 1895.

THE HUMAN RELATIONS AREA FILES

The Human Relations Area Files contain carefully selected source materials, analyzed and categorized according to An Outline of Cultural Materials. Their use is explained in A Guide to the Use of the Files, to be found at each File. The Files are located at:

University of Chicago	University of North Carolina
University of Colorado	University of Oklahoma
Cornell University	University of Pennsylvania
Harvard University	Princeton University
University of Hawaii	University of Southern California
Indiana University	University of Utah
State University of Iowa	University of Washington
University of Michigan	Yale University

AN OUTLINE OF CULTURAL MATERIALS (OCM)

TABLE OF CONTENTS

The following table of contents serves as an index to the sequence of categories, about seven hundred in number, by which the data on man, his behavior, and his environment are systematically filed.

There are separate files for each distinctive culture or sub-culture and likewise for each major historical period in the case of societies with records extending over periods of substantial cultural change. The files of each participating institution are housed in filing cabinets accommodating paper slips of the dimensions 5" by 8".

Sources selected for processing are annotated according to the numbered categories of the OCM. Annotation divides the material into logical blocks averaging perhaps a paragraph in length. Such blocks normally contain information pertinent to several categories of the OCM.

Each page of a source is reproduced for filing as many times as there are different categories for which it has been annotated. Thus the files contain, not abstracts, but the literal content of each source processed. In addition, for each file, one copy of every page is placed in Category 116 (Texts). This brings together, in regular page order, the complete text of all sources analyzed. Foreign sources are reproduced both in the original and in translation.

PREFACE

10 ORIENTATION
101 Identification
102 Maps
103 Place Names
104 Glossary
105 Cultural Summary

11 BIBLIOGRAPHY
111 Sources Processed
112 Sources Consulted
113 Additional References
114 Comments
115 Informants
116 Texts
117 Field Data

12 METHODOLOGY
121 Theoretical Orientation
122 Practical Preparations
123 Observational Role
124 Interviewing
125 Tests and Schedules
126 Recording
127 Historical Research
128 Organization of Results

13 GEOGRAPHY
131 Location
132 Climate
133 Topography
134 Soil
135 Mineral Resources
136 Fauna
137 Flora

14 HUMAN BIOLOGY
141 Anthropometry
142 Descriptive Somatology
143 Genetics
144 Racial Affinities

145 Ontogenetic Data
146 Nutrition
147 Physiological Data

15 BEHAVIOR PROCESSES AND PERSONALITY
151 Sensation and Perception
152 Drives and Emotions
153 Modification of Behavior
154 Adjustment Processes
155 Personality
156 Social Personality
157 Personality Traits
158 Personality Disorders
159 Life History Materials

16 DEMOGRAPHY
161 Population
162 Composition of Population
163 Birth Statistics
164 Morbidity
165 Mortality
166 Internal Migration
167 Immigration and Emigration
168 Population Policy

17 HISTORY AND CULTURE CHANGE
171 Distributional Evidence
172 Archeology
173 Traditional History
174 Historical Reconstruction
175 Recorded History
176 Innovation
177 Acculturation
178 Socio-Cultural Trends

18 TOTAL CULTURE
181 Ethos
182 Function
183 Norms
184 Cultural Participation
185 Cultural Goals

417 Apparatus

42 PROPERTY
421 Property System
422 Property in Movables
423 Real Property
424 Incorporated Property
425 Acquisition & Relinquish-
   ment of Property
426 Borrowing and Lending
427 Renting and Leasing
428 Inheritance
429 Administration

43 EXCHANGE
431 Gift Giving
432 Buying and Selling
433 Production and Supply
434 Income and Demand
435 Price and Value
436 Medium of Exchange
437 Exchange Transactions
438 Domestic Trade
439 Foreign Trade

44 MARKETING
441 Mercantile Business
442 Wholesale Marketing
443 Retail Marketing
444 Retail Businesses
445 Service Industries
446 Sales Promotion
447 Advertising

45 FINANCE
451 Accounting
452 Credit
453 Banking
454 Saving and Investment
455 Speculation
456 Insurance
457 Foreign Exchange

458 Business Cycles

46 LABOR
461 Labor and Leisure
462 Division of Labor by Sex
463 Occupational Specialization
464 Labor Supply and Employment
465 Wages and Salaries
466 Labor Relations
467 Labor Organization
468 Collective Bargaining

47 BUSINESS AND INDUSTRIAL
ORGANIZATION
471 Ownership and Control of
   Capital
472 Individual Enterprise
473 Corporate Organization
474 Cooperative Organization
475 State Enterprise
476 Mutual Aid
477 Competition

48 TRAVEL AND TRANSPORTATION
481 Locomotion
482 Burden Carrying
483 Weight Moving
484 Travel
485 Travel Services
486 Regulation of Travel
487 Routes
488 Warehousing
489 Transportation

49 LAND TRANSPORT
491 Highways
492 Animal Transport
493 Vehicles
494 Highway Transport
495 Auxiliary Highway Services
496 Railways
497 Rail Transport

734 Invalidism
735 Poverty
736 Dependency
737 Old Age Dependency
738 Delinquency

74 HEALTH AND WELFARE
741 Philanthropic Foundations
742 Medical Research
743 Hospitals and Clinics
744 Public Health and Sanitation
745 Social Insurance
746 Public Assistance
747 Private Welfare Agencies
748 Social Work

75 SICKNESS
751 Preventive Medicine
752 Bodily Injuries
753 Theory of Disease
754 Sorcery
755 Magical and Mental Therapy
756 Psychotherapists
757 Medical Therapy
758 Medical Care
759 Medical Personnel

76 DEATH
761 Life and Death
762 Suicide
763 Dying
764 Funeral
765 Mourning
766 Deviant Mortuary Practices
767 Mortuary Specialists
768 Social Readjustments to
    Death
769 Cult of the Dead

77 RELIGIOUS BELIEFS
771 General Character of
    Religion

772 Cosmology
773 Mythology
774 Animism
775 Eschatology
776 Spirits and Gods
777 Luck and Chance
778 Sacred Objects and Places
779 Theological Systems

78 RELIGIOUS PRACTICES
781 Religious Experience
782 Propitiation
783 Purification and Expiation
784 Avoidance and Taboo
785 Asceticism
786 Orgies
787 Revelation and Divination
788 Ritual
789 Magic

79 ECCLESIASTICAL ORGANIZATION
791 Magicians and Diviners
792 Holy Men
793 Priesthood
794 Congregations
795 Sects
796 Organized Ceremonial
797 Missions
798 Religious Persecution

80 NUMBERS AND MEASURES
801 Numerology
802 Numeration
803 Mathematics
804 Weights and Measures
805 Ordering of Time

81 EXACT KNOWLEDGE
811 Logic
812 Philosophy
813 Scientific Method
814 Humanistic Studies

HRAF PRESS

SURVEY OF WORLD CULTURES

Jordan, George L. Harris and others. Pp. 256; illus.; tables; bibliography. 1958. $5.50.

Poland, Clifford R. Barnett and others. Pp. 448; illus.; tables; bibliography. 1958. $7.50.

COUNTRY SERIES

Afghanistan, Donald N. Wilber and others. Pp. xii, 501; illus.; tables; bibliography. 1956. $8.75.

Cambodia, David J. Steinberg and others. Pp. xii, 345; illus.; tables; bibliography. 1957. $7.75.

Egypt, George L. Harris and others. Pp. xii, 370; illus.; tables; bibliography. 1957. $8.00.

Iran, Herbert H. Vreeland and others. Pp. viii, 347; illus.; tables; bibliography. 1957. $8.00.

North Borneo, Brunei, Sarawak (British Borneo), George L. Harris and others. Pp. xi, 287; illus.; tables; bibliography. 1956. $6.00.

RSFSR (Russian Soviet Federated Socialist Republic), Thomas Fitzsimmons and others. 2 vols. Pp. xii, 681; illus.; tables; bibliography. 1957. $9.75.

COUNTRY SERIES

Thailand, Wendell Blanchard and others. Pp. 525; illus. ; tables; bibliography. 1958. $6.50.

BEHAVIOR SCIENCE BIBLIOGRAPHIES

Selected Bibliography of the Philippines, Fred Eggan and others. Pp. vi, 138. 1956. $3.75.

Southeast Asia: Selected Annotated Bibliography of Japanese Publications, James K. Irikura. Pp. xii, 544. 1956. $8.50.

Paleosiberian Peoples and Languages: A Bibliographical Guide, Roman Jakobson and others. Pp. viii, 222. 1957. $5.50.

Bibliography of Indonesian Peoples and Cultures, Raymond Kennedy. (2d ed., revised.) 2 vols. Pp. xxviii, 663. 1955. $8.50.

Jordan, Lebanon and Syria: An Annotated Bibliography, Raphael Patai. Pp. vii, 289. 1957. $6.50.

Selected Bibliography on the Geography of Southeast Asia, Part III: Malaya, Karl J. Pelzer. Pp. iv, 162. 1956. $2.50.

Annotated Bibliography of Burma, Frank N. Trager and others. Pp. viii, 230. 1956. $5.75.

Japanese and Chinese Language Sources on Burma: An Annotated Bibliography, Frank N. Trager and others. Pp. x, 122. 1957. $3.50.

Annotated Bibliography of Afghanistan, Donald N. Wilber. Pp. ix, 220. 1956. $5.50.

Economic and Social Development of Modern China: A Bibliographical Guide, Tung-Li Yuan. Part I, pp. viii, 130; Part II, pp. v, 87. 1956. $5.50.

BEHAVIOR SCIENCE MONOGRAPHS

An Atoll Culture: Ethnography of Ifaluk in the Central Carolines, Edwin
G. Burrows and Melford E. Spiro. (2d ed.) Pp. xvi, 355; illus.;
tables; bibliography. 1957. $4.50.

Double Descent Among the Fanti, James Boyd Christensen. Pp. xiii,
145; illus.; bibliography. 1954. $2.50.

The Eastern Carolines, John L. Fischer and Ann M. Fischer. Pp. xiv,
274; illus.; tables; bibliography. 1957. $6.50.

Pakistan: Society and Culture, Stanley Maron and others. Pp. ix, 192;
illus.; bibliography. 1957. $3.50.

Mongol Community and Kinship Structure, Herbert Harold Vreeland, III.
(2d ed.) Pp. xi, 359; illus.; tables; bibliography. 1957. $3.50.

BEHAVIOR SCIENCE OUTLINES

Outline of Cultural Materials, George P. Murdock and others. (3d ed.,
revised.) Pp. xxiii, 162. 1950. $2.50.

Outline of South American Cultures, George P. Murdock. Pp. 148; illus.;
bibliography. 1951. $2.50.

Outline of World Cultures, George P. Murdock. Pp. xii, 180. 1954. $3.00.

BEHAVIOR SCIENCE REPRINTS

The Indian Village Community, B. H. Baden-Powell. (1st ed. 1896.)
Pp. xvi, 456; tables; bibliography. $3.95.

The Melanesians: Studies in Their Anthropology and Folk-Lore, R. H.
Codrington. (1st ed. 1891.) Pp. xv, 419; illus. 1957. $3.95.

League of the Ho-de-no-sau-nee or Iroquois, Lewis H. Morgan. (Ed.,
H. M. Lloyd, 1901.) Vol. I, pp. xx, 338; Vol. II, pp. xii, 332;
illus.; tables; bibliography. 1954. $7.50.

BEHAVIOR SCIENCE REPRINTS

The Sanpoil and Nespelem: Salishan Peoples of Northeastern Washington, Verne F. Ray. (1st ed. 1933.) Pp. 237; illus.; tables; bibliography. 1954. $2.50.

BEHAVIOR SCIENCE TRANSLATIONS

Among the Samoyed in Siberia, Kai Donner. Pp. xx, 176; illus. 1954. $2.50.

Persian Beliefs and Customs, Henri Masse. Pp. xiii, 516; illus.; bibliography. 1954. $4.75.

Snow People (Chukchee), Taeki Odulok. Pp. xvii, 73. 1954. $2.00.

The Mewu-Fantzu: A Tibetan Tribe of Kansu, Hans Stubel. Pp. viii, 63; bibliography. 1957. $2.75.